God Didn't Make The Ape

A Second Look at Where They Came From

By Steve Preston

3rd Edition

© Copyright 2015
All rights reserved.
No part of this book may be reproduced, stored in a retrieval system, or transmitted by any means, electronic, mechanical, photocopying, recording, or otherwise, without written permission from the author.

Table of Contents

God Didn't Make The Ape 1
Introduction 4
In The Beginning 12
Radioactive Decay Variations 17
Ice Core Dating 19
Ape DNA 29
Four Views Of Evolution 32
Man Evolved 39
Normal Evolution Studies 41
Search for a Servant 44
Descriptions of Man's Beginnings 47
Biblical History 67
Book Of Secrets 71
"The Book of Giants" 74
Aegyptopithecus 76
Australopithecus 77
Homo-Habilis 79
Homo Erectus 81
Neanderthal 84
Gigantopithecus Ape-Man 91
Meganthropus Ape-man 96
Evidence Of Ancient Engineers 100
Batteries, Growing Blocks and Nuclear Plants 110
Scientists Push Evolution 117
Timeline That Fits 127
Consensus of Evolution 129
Experiments on Animals 134
Mutant Dragons 141
New Dinosaurs 145
War and Mutation 150
8 Major Mutations 157

More Dinosaurs *158*
Tower of Babel War *161*
South American Evidence *165*
Vanara People *170*
Vanara, Egypt and Electricity *175*
More Ape-Men Heroes *181*
Where Are the Ape-men Now? *186*
Devolved Humans *189*
Cross Breeding *198*
Conclusions *206*
About The Author *208*

Introduction

Let me tell you a story that will sound somewhat crazy. While this story seems fanciful, I will provide you with the evidence you need to believe what they told you in school was pretty much a lie. In this story, man lived with the dinosaurs and gained great civilizations only to have them fail as unimaginable war ensued. Hundreds of huge human footprints alongside massive dinosaur footprints have been found at ancient beach sites around the world including the United States, Europe, Central America, and Australia. As these giant humans, called Homo-Gigantus or Titan people walked, the beach filled sediments into the footprints to build images still extant and the same thing happened when dinosaurs went to the same beaches. I would suppose some people walked too slowly and were trampled, but that is a different story. Just about all would face the effects of war.

Cretaceous Extinction

We may not know the actual events, but soon the Earth was filled with destruction and the dinosaurs lay dead. Finally, a massive meteor crashed down and caused even more destruction. The earth split open to create the country of India as hundreds of thousands of **cubic miles** of magma spewed out placing a layer of iridium dust around the whole planet. Destabilized, the earth shifted on its axis and all the cities of the mighty people were completely destroyed.

From out of nowhere mighty humans, now called the Nephilim or Anak people, returned to reclaim the land, but misery ensued as the Tertiary Era started with nothing. While a number of animals survived and thrived, the Anak scientists worked to relieve the suffering in many ways. One way was to modify the various animals. The Anak people got good at modifying animals and even <u>made what we call Apes</u>. Experiment after experiment built on the beginning until a man-like ape called Australpithicus was developed. We are told in Judeo-Christian texts that the creator God would <u>call all the modified animals unclean or abominations</u>.

All of a sudden a new man we call Homo-Erectus appeared in Africa. Homo Erectus was different as he was made by the creator God. Some Anak people continued to modify the various animals and even modified the DNA of Homo-Erectus Man. It should be noted that during this time there were no Chimpanzees or Bonobo and the world was dominated by the Anak people. The Anak experiments had modified Homo-Erectus and produced many variants of humans including the Neanderthal humans who had larger brains than modern humans.

The Pleistocene Age [40 to 10 thousand years ago]

From nowhere the Cro-Magnon Man species just appeared one day in the Middle East. This was approximately 40 thousand years ago which identified the beginning of the Pleistocene Age. We are told that these people looked like modern man, but they had a slightly larger brain than the Neanderthal and they were very creative and warlike. This new human also learned how to modify animals just like the Anak. Between the Anak and Cro-Magnon, additional animals were manufactured and even more dinosaurs were remade less than 30 thousand years ago. Civilization had again amassed greatness, but war took away luxury and death eliminated happiness. Nuclear material from processing plants in Oklo, Africa was used for weaponry around the world and massive mutation of DNA in Cro-Magnon man was noted at this time 11 thousand years ago. To top it all off, massive meteor showers peppered much of the landscape after something happened to the planet Venus [known as Rahab by the Biblical writers]. Apparently its moon exploded and the planet was almost split in half as its atmosphere, life, and beauty all was gone in an instant. Hundreds of thousands of meteors struck the Earth along the coastline of what would be the United States and around the other side of the world in Australia. Massive fires overtook the landscape and flooding destroyed many just before the end of the Pleistocene.

Pleistocene Extinction [10 thousand Years Ago]

Things seems to be sort of "ok" for a little while but it wasn't long before the earth stability once again could not maintain its normal spin and it shifted on its axis by about 30 degrees, 10 thousand years ago. Wooly Mammoths eating flowers in a meadow, found their meadow in the Arctic and they quickly froze to death. The atmosphere shifted wildly. The ice at the poles melted. The rains came and all was lost as the Pleistocene Extinction almost destroyed the world again. Some survivors on various boats and vehicle weathered the massive storms but the horrors of the shift caused Cro-Magnon and Anak survivors to cry out in anguish according to Biblical and Sumerian historical documents. Apes had changed substantially during the Tertiary and Pleistocene Age, but the Chimpanzee and Bonobo still were not in existence.

The Bharata War [3500-3100BC]

Soon great civilizations again peppered the landscape. Modern conveniences like indoor plumbing and toilets found in great cities like Mohen-jo-Daro and the cities of the

PreInca attested to a life of comfort, but war again would take control of life itself. Again the nuclear weapons built with products from the ancient Oklo processing plants provided both escalation and death. Many around the world were driven underground with some underground cities hold many thousands hoping the outside wars would soon end. We are told, 1/3 of all the inhabitants of the world died during the exchanges and something else. As the war ended, the Egyptians called the ending Zep-Tepi [a new beginning], In India the Age of Kali began. The PreMaya started a new 5000 year calendar at the end of the war and the earth was in shambles.

Zep Tepi [3100BC]

We find more major mutations in human DNA than any other time. About ½ of all major mutations of humans occurred during the war years. The book of Jasher indicated that massive numbers <u>became like apes</u> as we entered a new Stone Age existence. People had changed as many new races emerged. Those greatly affected looked more animal than human. Indian literature called this group of people the Vanara. This group would not survive long, but another mutation was responsible for 2 new Apes as mutation spawned both the chimpanzee and bonobos from humans and this has been known for some time now.

Book Overview

This book is about monkeys, gibbons, marmosets, humans, apes, Ape-men, and humans. Of interest is the one we call chimpanzee. While you have been told that men evolved from apes, there is no science describing how that would happen and the DNA of a gorilla that were supposedly sprang from is substantially different than human DNA. We can believe Australopithicus and even Homo-Habilis DNA would show more similarity to Gorilla than to humans but no DNA has been found.

Law of Entropy

Some misguided "consensus researchers" try to hold on to Evolution and survival of the fittest to develop higher levels of beings, but the Law of Entropy would never allow a more developed animal to survive over a "devolved entity". Advancing a species can only be assumed when an outside force specifically controls the modification of DNA to establish a "Higher Level" of animal. I know this is not making sense and it's by no means completely correct either, but it addresses many anomalies, errors, and limitations of what you were taught in school concerning the development of Apes and man. This book will generally trace the development of man's closest relatives, but along the way other animals will have to be addressed because they also play a part in this overview.

The Bible calls the ape an abomination. While that seems strange, it may help us here.

Abomination

Some Biblical translations change the word abomination to UNCLEAN to confuse people, but the animals were not unclean, they were simply considered abominable by our creator God. There is a very good reason that he thought of them as abominations and the answer will be forthcoming. Later, about 6 thousand years ago, something remarkable and fearful happened. The book of Jasher says it with a simple phrase that I mentioned before.

"Some Men became "like" an Ape"

The book will also get into the de-evolution of men after what was called the Aryan Invasion [Persians], or the Babel War [Jewish Holy Men], or the Bharata War [Dravidian

Indians], or the War leading to Zep-Tepi [Khemetian Egyptians]. It will not be pleasant. Let's see what the ancient book of "Jasher" had to say [paraphrased].

> *The consequences of the building of the Babel Tower and Citadel, 6 thousand years ago, was that 1/3 of the people in the world would die in war, 1/3 would be changed into apes and elephants, and the remaining people would lose many of the capabilities they previously had and they would scatter to the ends of the world.*

I'm not getting into the elephant part in this book, but we find evidence of the ape-like people everywhere. During this same time period great works of art, documents, and ancient descriptions from around the world describe some of the people as being ape-like, as the entire world was thrust back into a second Stone Age for a time. The Egyptian god Thoth was depicted as ape-like as were the hero Hanuman from Indian historical references and the Aztec demi-god named Quetzalcoatl. I think that this is strange enough for an investigation so we certainly will look at that later.

Odd Monkey DNA

Scientists found out that the number of DNA modifications in a Chimpanzee are more than the modification number associated with man. Curiously, that means that at least some apes were "evolved" **from mankind**. How weird is that!!! I'm putting that on the list of things to investigate as well so that we can get to the bottom of this commonly misrepresented theme. The map below shows that monkeys and apes had the same ancestral beginning locations as all hominids, so let's look to see how each of the later apes came about. The chart to the right shows the genus and what came first, but let me expand on that just a little.

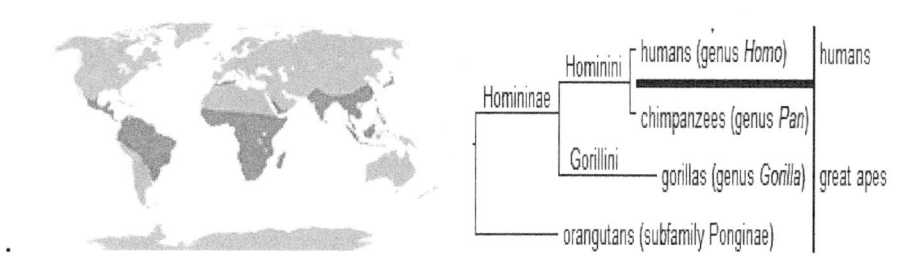

Homo Sapien Family Homininae- This group includes Homo Habilis and Rudalfensis, but traces of alien DNA believed to have been from Habilis were found in human species Homo Floresienesis, Heidelberg, and Denisovan with dates as recent as 12,000 years ago. This shows gorilla pulled away from the human species somewhere between 100 and 80 thousand years ago. OK! I know you have been told the homo-habilis was part man and part ape, but the differences are so extensive, the change to Homo-Erectus man could not have been accomplished. I know the Habilis has 2 eyes, 2 nose holes, 2 ears, 2 lungs, 2 legs, 2 arms, and many other things that say its human. ---Wait just a minute! That could identify thousands of different animals. It is becoming clear that homo-habilis was an animal. I'll go over the details of how this guy got here as part of this work so that you will have a more complete picture of monkeys and other apes and that brings us to the Hominini.

Homo Sapien Family Hominini – This is the true human including Homo-Erectus, Australopithecus, Georgicus, Antecessor, and Neanderthal. From this tree we can believe chimpanzee came on the scene between 80 and 5 thousand years ago. Many say they came along during the Pleistocene, but that may not be the only possibility. In fact, it is highly unlikely.

Let me start at the beginning.

In The Beginning

While this is not a book on religion, we will look at historical records, physical evidence and scientific research as well as religious documents together to understand how the Apes got here. As uncontrolled evolution cannot make things more complex, we can assume that the Big Bang and all the other elements associated with the beginning had an outside influence. For this initial section we will look at the little book of Genesis in the Judeo-Christian Bible to help us establish the needed outside influence. The word BARA in the first verse specifies the making of something from nothing. Don't let anyone tell you that "created from nothing" ["BARA] and "made" ['ASAH] are the same thing. Hebrew would not have 2 separate words for the same thing. They simply did not have that many words. In the first 23 verses we find our Creator God created the world, it was destroyed and then he started creating a new world. The "first 5 Ages" or "YOWMs" after the destruction are described in these first verses.

Day and Age are Interchangeable-Biblical Translations many times use the term "day" for YOWM like "day of harvest", or "day of suffering", or "day of famine" etc. found throughout the Bible. While day is the correct translation, it in no way is related to 24 hours in fact the first 3 "YOWMs" in Genesis occur before the earth and Sun were placed where they are today. I'm not getting into Anthropic and Relativistic Science in this book, so let's leave this confusing discussion alone and get to some meat.

Genesis 1:1-23 *In the beginning God "BARA/created" the Heavens, Earth. HAYAH/Then the Earth <u>became without form and void.</u> Afterwards He created the stars, sun, moon, firmament, great whales, sea creatures, and every winged fowl.*

Other books tell us more about the destruction described as it marks an extinction of the Earth we all know about, the Cretaceous Extinction. Here are just a few of the Judeo-Christian descriptions, but there are multitudes of texts from around the world describing the "War of the Giants and Gods."

Jeremiah 4:23-24*-[near the end of the war] "I beheld the Earth, and, I beheld, and, lo, there was no man, and all <u>the cities</u> thereof were broken down for thus hath the LORD said, the <u>whole land shall be desolate;</u>* [If the cities were broken down, there must have been cities before the war.]

Isaiah 9 and 13---`*Is this the man [Satan and his army] who made the Earth tremble, who shook kingdoms, who <u>made the world like a desert and overthrew its cities</u>, All the kings of the nations lie in glory, each in his own tomb; but you are cast out [from heaven to live on Earth again showing these were the Anak people]. They come from a far country, <u>from the end of heaven, even the LORD, and the weapons of his indignation, to destroy the whole land</u>* [<u>and make it without form and void</u>].

Enoch II 28: 3- *One of the angels "Satan" gathered angels against God and was kicked out of heaven* [and was abandoned to Earth again as these guys became the Anak people.]

Enoch 1:5-7. *And all shall be smitten with fear And the Watchers* [Rebel Angels that were Satan's army] *shall quake, And great fear and trembling shall seize them unto the ends of the earth. And the high mountains shall be shaken, And the* *high hills shall be made low, And shall melt like wax before the flame <u>And the earth shall be rent in sunder, And all that is upon the earth shall perish,</u>*

Then Moses said something different so we can believe that many of the creatures during the Tertiary and Pleistocene were modifications of Gods creations. This will be the case for many modified animals.

Genesis 1:24-And God said "<u>**Let the Earth** bring forth</u> cattle and beasts.

As we continue we find that others [we know from other verses that these were the Anak] besides God was modifying animals. They even were trying to make a man. The second sentence says God had to step in and create a man. We believe this was Homo-Erectus made during the 6th YOWM/Age after the Cretaceous Extinction about 100 thousand years ago. [I know you were told it was 2 million years ago, but the different date will be explained later.]

Genesis 1:25-28-And <u>they</u> said; Let <u>us</u> make man in our image. So the God created man in <u>his</u> own image. [This was done in the 6th Age after the War].

Jasher 1:1 And the gods said, Let <u>us</u> make [ASAH] man in our image, after <u>our</u> likeness, [This must have not been satisfactory so---] *God created man in his own image.*

Then something strange was written again as Moses said God wanted them to <u>replenish the earth</u> since it had been decimated from war. This of course means there were people on the earth before the war, during the Mesozoic Era.

Genesis 1:29-30-*God said unto them [***Homo Erectus** *people]*. <u>**Re-plenish**</u> *the Earth, and subdue it:*

We even get a description about what the first people and the Anak people looked like.

Baruch 3:26 - *There were the giants famous **from the beginning**, that were of so great stature.* [**Homo-Gigantus** people of the Mesozoic Era]

Genesis 6:4 *There were giants* [**Homo-Gigantus** people of the Mesozoic Era] *in the earth in those days; and also after that, when the sons of God* [Those who became the **Anak** people] *came in unto the daughters of men, and they bare children to them, the same became Giants* [Giant children came from Anak who were giants like Homo-Gigantus]

The Anak Survived the Worldwide Flood

Later we find that a substantial number of Anak people survived the Pleistocene Extinction. When the Jews left Egypt in 1560BC they saw Anak giants everywhere in the land of Canaan. They were so huge the Jews thought they would look like grasshoppers to them. One of these guys was killed by Moses. He was King of Bashan his name was Og, and he was 11 feet tall. In North America, hundreds of giant corpses have been found, many around 11 feet tall and one was described as being 17 feet tall. Many of these skeletons were dated to after the flood as well.

Chapter One Essence

In chapter one, more than just the planet was made in fact, many now believe that the 1st verse of Genesis covers the entire time from the beginning when the earth was initially formed until the end of the Cretaceous Age when the dinosaurs died and the earth became void and without form due to a massive, horrible, devastating and criminal war that took place on the Earth and other worlds including a place called Heaven. To weird you out more, civilized people lived on the earth during some portion of this time and some of these people were genetic scientists. ----I'm not loony on this!! There is a tremendous amount of evidence to support this whole thing and I will provide some of those details shortly. Before getting into the second chapter, let me just say that the first account is of <u>life during the Mesozoic Era</u> [Dinosaurs] on the Earth. What you need to know here is that civilized people lived during this time. The Greeks called them the <u>Titans</u> and some modern scientists call them Homo-Gigantus. No matter, around the world we find that these first people "created" animals by genetics. The animals ACTUALLY created by the Creator God were <u>considered Clean</u> to him and those MANIPULATED by the Titans were considered <u>Abominations</u> or unclean. After a time the Titans died and became something we call the watchers and because they were "dead" their existence was in a different universe called Heaven. I don't want to get into why our universe cannot exist without a symbiotic universe like Heaven being linked to us, but there is no doubt that heaven exists. Anyway: some of them did not like it there and a war was started. As a result of the war, those who revolted became human again and were called the Annunaki [by the Sumerians], Olympian gods [by the Greeks], the Anak [by the Jews], the Akamim [by the Mongulala in Brazil] or Asa [by many African Tribes] and Archaics [by the Adena and Ojibwa of North America]. The important part of all this is that the Anak liked to create animals from other animals. One of the animals they loved to modify we call primate. I know this doesn't make sense right now, but I have a substantial amount of evidence. Right now let me get back to Genesis and switch to the 2nd verse.

God Rested

After God Created Homo-Erectus he sat back and watched for a time during what is called the 7th Age.

Genesis 2:1-2-And on the seventh "Age" God ended His work which He had made; and He rested.

Cro-Magnon Created

Next Moses tells us he finished resting around the beginning of the Pleistocene Age to CREATE a more useful man. [Cro-Magnon]

***Genesis 2:7-8**-And the <u>LORD God</u> [The Creator] formed man of the dust of the ground, and breathed into his nostrils the breath of life; and man <u>became a living soul</u>. And the "LORD God" [The Creator] planted a garden eastward in Eden, and there He put the man whom He had formed.*

To some; all this is sounding pretty stupid, after all, in school you were told the Tertiary Period started 65 million years ago, so times don't add up. The problem is that previously we relied on nuclear decay to tell us how old things were including how old our Earth was. Today we know radioactive decay timing is grossly in error. Before we go on, let me sort of retime the Earth for you.

Radioactive Decay Variations

Solar Flare Variation-The majority of geologists today tell you that radiometric dating has narrowed the age of Earth to about 4.5 billion years, give or take a couple of percent. We now know that is hogwash and science is refining the timing more and more each day. The Earth and everything in it is much younger. I don't mean the Earth is only 6 thousand years old as some have suggested, but let's see the evidence. Researchers at Purdue and Stanford have found evidence that radio decay rates are not constant at all. On December 13, 2006, a magnificent solar flare flung radiation and solar particles toward Earth. Measuring the decay rate of manganese-54 during the flare proved to be very interesting as the decay rate dropped during the time of the radiation fallout. It was determined that solar neutrinos zipped through space and affected Mn-54's decay rates used in the experiment. Just think about this. They were testing a single solar flare event and the change was significant. The sun has these things all the time.

Seasonal Variation-It was also found that the decay rates of silicon-32 and radium-226 showed seasonal variation, according to data collected at Brookhaven National Laboratory on Long Island and the Federal Physical and Technical Institute in Germany. This error was just the material sitting there with almost no outside interference.

Just Plane Different-Wood buried in igneous rock in Queensland Australia has been dated to 40 thousand years, while the basalt around it dated to 45 million years. Both dating subjects should have given the same date, since the igneous rock was formed at the same time the wood was buried. Many of the "data-ologists" don't tell you about major errors like this.

Lava Errors- Excess argon-36 was found in three out of 26 lava flows in recent times. So Argon/argon testing would show a much older date that actually was "KNOWN" This is believed to be because there was too much of the argon-36 in the first place. In Grand Canyon lava flow testing, it showed lower levels of lava were younger than the top layers. At different volcano sites, that had eruption in 1949, 1954 and 1975; the same thing was noted. These samples were dated by Geochron Laboratories of Cambridge, Massachusetts. Even though the oldest of these samples are just over sixty-years old, the lab tests provided ages that ranged from 270,000 years to 3.5 million years old. Additionally, we go to Mt. St. Helens and its eruptions in the 1980's. Samples there gave old ages in the range of 300,000 to 2.7 million years. Hopefully, you are beginning to see that we know less about how old we are than you believed before reading this.

Just imagine the Nuclear decay tells you a date but it is known it can be off by 10 thousand percent or so. Unfortunately, all the books have been written, evolution graphs have been analyzed, lecturers have been lauded, and "survival of the fittest overviews" have made researchers famous.

Distance to the Sun-If neutrinos from a single solar flare can make things look older, what if the entire Earth was closer to the sun? I know that sounds odd, so just keep it in the back of your mind right now as we look at Ice Core Testing. I'll be getting back to the sun distance in a while.

Ice Core Dating

Although the task is tedious, ice can be examined just like tree rings. Each summer ice changes its consistency. $H_2O(16)$ is more concentrated in the summer while $H_2O(18)$ is more concentrated in the winter. This gives us indication to the level of CO2 which in turn allows us to understand something about the temperature levels. As the yearly cycle has freezing and thawing, ice consistency varies each day, seasonally, and yearly, depending on Earth axis and other critical elements. Anyway, scientists around the world started boring holes in ice. Most coring is done in Greenland and Antarctica and a sample is shown below.

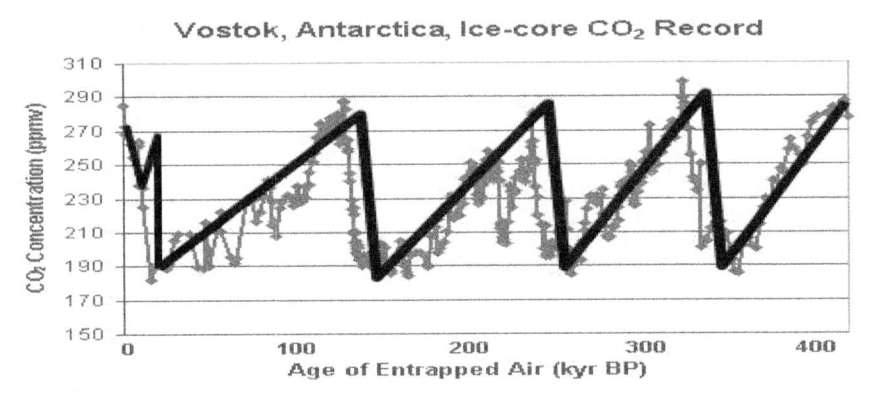

Vostok, Antarctica, Ice-core CO_2 Record

[Graph showing CO_2 Concentration (ppmv) on y-axis from 150 to 310, and Age of Entrapped Air (kyr BP) on x-axis from 0 to 400]

Notice, every 100 thousand or so years, there is a MASSIVE change in the CO_2 concentration or temperature associated to some massive change. One would think this type of change would kill animals, so we might be able to use the Ice core to give us a different timeline that is better characterized by physical evidence around the world.

Before we leave this chart, please notice a sharp rise about 11 thousand years ago followed by a dip around 10 thousand years ago which indicates 2 massive climate changes occurred within a relatively short time. Yes, I know there is one of these things 220 thousand years ago, but for the study of Apes, the more recent ones are of more importance.

Greenland Check-From the next chart, we can see a correlation in near term events. Eleven or 12 thousand years ago a major spike in temperature with a fast cooling followed by another just a few thousand years later then an almost flat plateau where Greenland's temperature has not changed and Greenland's position relative to the axis of spin has been unchanged. Before that time, it seems, the temperature was generally colder with what looks like a rise in temperature starting around 100 thousand years ago.

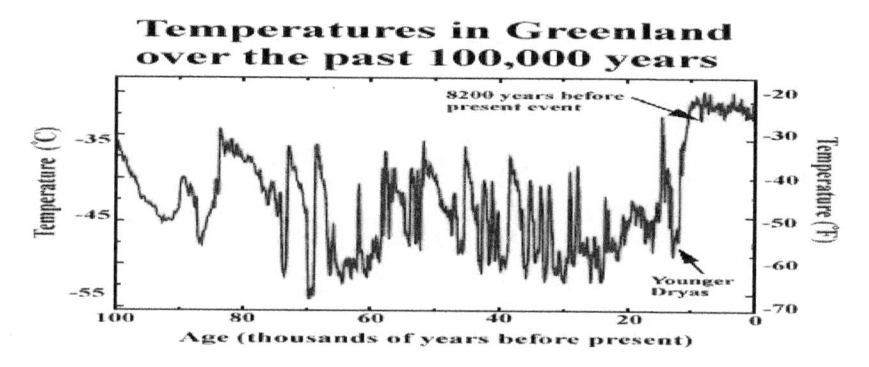

Temperatures in Greenland over the past 100,000 years

8200 years before present event

Younger Dryas

Age (thousands of years before present)

Paleo-Magnetics to the Rescue-The Atlantic Ocean is getting wider about an inch a year, averaged worldwide. While the building of the great mountains has little to do with the normal tectonic plate "drift" We can pretty accurately measure the widening ocean in various ways including measuring distances between matched magnetic landmarks on either side of a widening gap on the ocean floor. The Old theory indicated that 180 million years ago the continent Pangea began splitting apart and has been drifting ever since. In so doing, the landmasses of the Western and Eastern hemispheres separated and opened the Atlantic Ocean basin today.

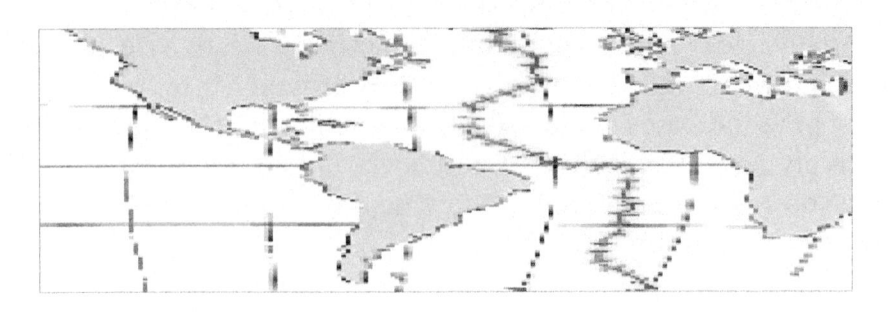

Plate tectonics tells us the outer hard crust of Earth consists actually of a dozen or so distinct, hard plates that drift individually on hot, deformable rock. An unequal distribution of heat within Earth moves the plates. The boundary between the plates forming the Atlantic Ocean is smack down the middle along the Mid-Atlantic Ridge, shown as the hashed line in the figure above. The ridge is where we must look to find a widening gap, which accounts for the widening ocean. That is where we measure the rate of separation. Where the plates separate, white-hot soft mantle oozes up from great depths within the Earth to fill the gap. The molten rock cools slowly into new slivers of sea floor. This happened over and over again through the eons. That's how the Atlantic Ocean widened-by a spreading sea floor. We measure the gap rate in various ways including direct measurements of plate movement using satellite images. Another is the Paleo-magnetic method. As the Earth's magnetic poles reverse polarity periodically, the North Pole becomes the South Pole and vice versa and much of the magma spewing out is iron.

Iron-rich rock has a peculiar property: heat it above its curie point of 580 degrees Centigrade and it loses its magnetism. When it cools the rock gets re-magnetized in the direction of the existing Earth's magnetic field. So it's a magnet with the poles aligning with the poles of the Earth at the time of the cooling. The neat thing about this is: the magnetic field of the rock, once cooled, stays frozen in this orientation. It becomes a record of the Earth's field at the time of its cooling. To measure the rate of separation, we identify two slivers of sea floor on opposite sides of the ridge that have the same magnetic polarities frozen at the same time. If you know when these reversals occur, one can simply measure the distance between magnetic alignments of the ocean floor and one can determine the rate of expansion and how long ago Pangea began to separate. Unfortunately, if the initial time-base is wrong everything is skewed. With that, let's look at the center of the Atlantic Ocean. The graph following shows the last <u>14 flips over what was previously determined to be a period of 3.7 million years</u>. These figures came from Potassium-Argon [nuclear Decay] dating of magnetic material in solidified magma in the center of the Atlantic Ocean so we need to put the dating aside. Not only is a general time of each flip noted, but also the ferrous portions of the magma align with the magnetic field of the earth to show rotation of the earth over time. Another flip could happen any time. Using mathematical models of the external crust and inner molten material, researchers have estimated with mathematic models that the Earth should flip on its axis about every 100 thousand years. The problem with trying to determine the actual workings of the Earth is that no one has ever seen the inside of the Earth to model it properly, but the results do confirm the high possibility of a polar flip, which will cause mass destruction, tidal waves, and major climatic changes. With that scary introduction, let's look at the chart as it currently has been determined and understand that nuclear decay dating is not nearly as accurate as we once thought.

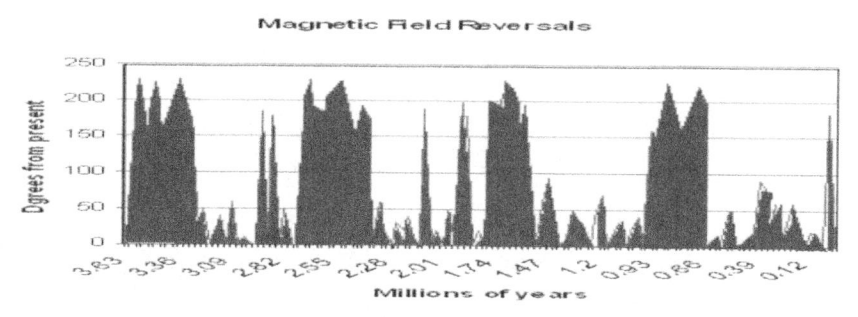

By this it shows massive shifts occurring 9, 12, 660, 930, 1470, 1740, 2260, 2550, and 3360 thousand years. They don't exactly match any of the "standard" extinction periods and they don't line up with Ice Core samples. They don't line up with anything, but if we compress the timeline, look at what we find!!

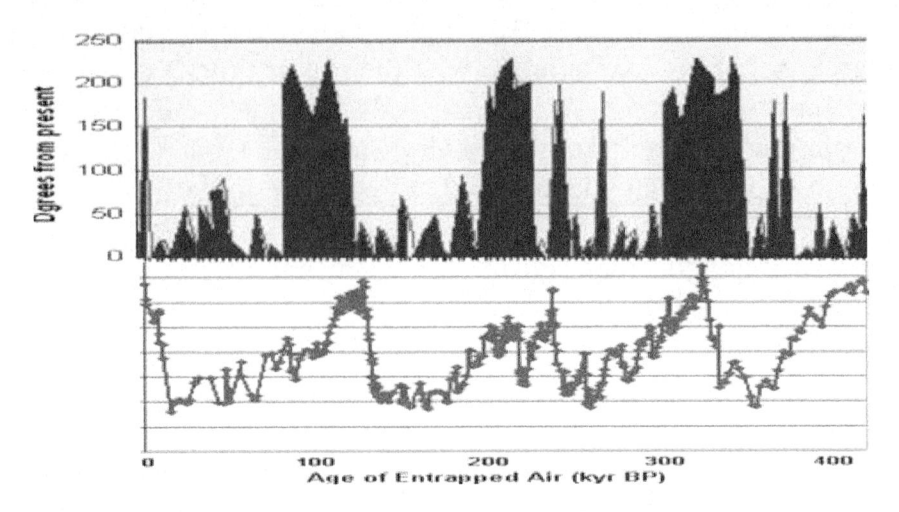

Changes in the earth axis seem to correlate very well with the data from the Ice core testing when the data is compressed. I know I haven't given you a real good reason to compress the data, but you certainly should recognize that the old data was substantially unreliable. Here is what you should recognize. The magnetic field reversals and the cyclic ice core CO_2 levels seem to have a repetitive, cyclic nature. Even that strange change around 230 thousand years ago seems to correlate with the mid Atlantic data. I need you to notice one more thing. The compressed timing gives us more substantiation for 2 major climactic events occurring within only a very short period of time around 10 thousand and 11 thousand years ago. Later I will describe details of these important markers that can be used to help reduce the predecessor timelines down to the more valid ones I am presenting here.

Plate Shifts-Like the magnetic shifts, major crust movements or earth axis positional changes have been estimated to happen about every 20,000 years. The most recent ones occurred 43,000, 22,000, and **10,000 years ago**. Sometimes the crust and magnetic field seems to wander over a number of years and other times it seems to jerk suddenly. One of the theories is that these "jerks" in the crust are apparently caused by the uneven weight of the various plates supported on the surface of the Earth; especially the 19 quadrillion tons of mass called Antarctica which is located at the present day South Pole. Each time a movement occurs, terrible things happen like tropical areas turning into glaciers. Whether the evidence shows magnetic field wander or plate shift wander doesn't really matter, because the outcome is the same.

Tropical Arctic-Researchers have found evidence that the Arctic was tropical for a short time, 100 thousand years ago, or so. They found bones of early crocodiles, turtles and fish that were all tropical and estimated the summer temperatures reached into the 90s. This could only mean that the plates shifted or the planet axis moved by a substantial amount. Finds similar to this have convinced many that the outer core of the Earth moves continually and that the movement is in jerks over time.

Tropical Antarctic-If we move to the other side of the world, we find the same thing. Swamp type dinosaur bones have been found along with remains of plants that existed before parts of Antarctica became extremely cold [the last time]. It seems the animals found would have been on earth around 100 thousand years ago according to the new timing. With that little piece of data, let's look at a very special timeline track called Hawaii. Hawaii hasn't always been where it is today. A record of its travels shows up as something called hot spots.

Hot Spot Dating

If the axis is changing, there should be some dramatic physical evidence and there is. The evidence is not only from the magnetic field alignments of molten material in the Atlantic Ocean, but also some easily seen evidence. The evidence is in the form of hot spots. The best hot spot to discuss is Hawaii. The volcanic action in Hawaii has nothing to do with the edges of the plates. The picture on the following page shows the basic outlines of the major plates and these anomalous "Hot Spots". The hot spots don't stay still. They wander, but they wander in straight lines interrupted by abrupt turns. By measuring the distance the "hot spot" travels, we can determine how long the Earth or a particular plate on the Earth stayed with a particular axis of rotation. The hot spots wander because the inner core is much denser than the outer core, and occasionally the two slip in the direction perpendicular to the axis of rotation. The reason we know the slippage is perpendicular is that it is still happening.

Plate Movement Direction-If we look at the apparent trail of the Hawaiian Islands over time, as shown below, a clear path is noted and times for each abrupt change has been approximated by distance. By the way, a new hotspot has just opened 73km south of the big island showing that the plate wander direction is still in the same direction as it has been over the last 10 thousand years and its perpendicular to the Earth rotational axis. With the distance between Midway and Hawaii known to be 1300 miles, the total distance of the hotspot track is about 4500 miles. Assuming the above timing is correct, the hotspot moves about ½ inches per year. While predecessor theories put the timing of the hotspot trail more spread out, new data has compressed the tack to agree with all the rest of the timing without the old nuclear decay standard. This makes the movement more like 50 feet per year.

Initially this sounds inappropriate as the Atlantic only increase in size about 1 inch per year today, but the motion of the hotspot has little to do with the expansion of the Atlantic Ocean as it is characterized by the differential between the Earth inside spin and the outside spin. Additionally, we get more proof of the information locked in this unusual hotspot motion by look other places. The Hawaiian Island chain isn't the only hot spot group that shows this pattern. Look on the following graphic left and see that two other hot spot wander directions in the Pacific Ocean look similar to that of the Hawaiian Island spot.

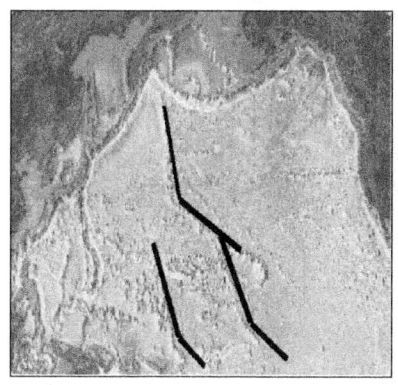

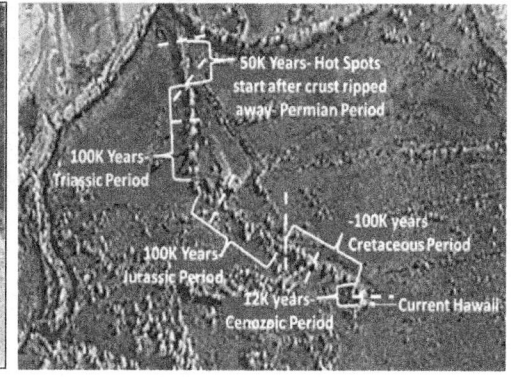

More Detail-I know you are thinking this is interesting, but it doesn't really help too much. So we have correlation of other hot spot trails and what seems to be timing compression similar to others used in this new light, but can the hot spots be traced back to the Antarctic Ice core? The answer can be seen in the next graphic. We know that the trails are produced perpendicular to the axis of rotation of the earth which is described as dotted lines below. If we that the changes in the earth axis at the apparent changes, we find something VERY interesting as shown next.

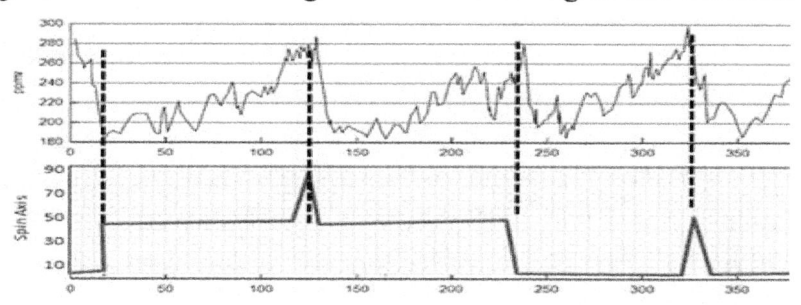

Notice that for a few thousand years about 100 thousand years ago Antarctica was probably warm between the Jurassic and Cretaceous Period. Sure enough animals from that time have been found under the ice---just sitting there waiting to be found. The graphic following tries to show some possible major earth "settling" points and general information about those spin axes. For instance, notice that the earth spin goes along the east coast of the United States 10 thousand years ago. This will be important later as we piece all of this together to try to see critical time marks to help us reevaluate the time line for us as humans.

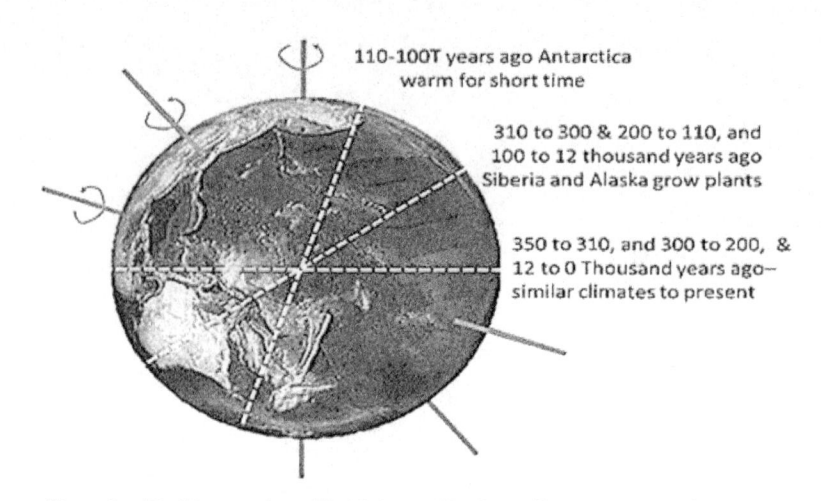

110-100T years ago Antarctica warm for short time

310 to 300 & 200 to 110, and 100 to 12 thousand years ago Siberia and Alaska grow plants

350 to 310, and 300 to 200, & 12 to 0 Thousand years ago– similar climates to present

Some Don't Believe in Shifting Poles-Some people try to infer that this whole thing about the Earth changing its axis is hogwash. Well, I think that there is just way too much data to assume otherwise. Antarctica with its dinosaur bones, the quick frozen Mammoths, the various polarities of the deposited iron from volcanic action in the middle of the Atlantic Ocean; they all tell the same story. The Earth axis can move and with it there can be relatively fast and devastating climatic changes. These changes are horrible, but may not be the responsible party for most of the extinction periods. The most effective exterminator on the Earth has been and will continue to be the Comet or Meteor. Whenever a comet or meteors hit and the earth axis shifts right afterwards, total chaos occurs as it did about 100 thousand years ago then 11 thousand years ago followed by another attack 10 thousand years ago. These 3 dates are important to us as humans. A hundred thousand years ago makes the extinction of most of the dinosaurs and most of the human race at that time. After the extinction, the Bible indicated that the earth was without form and void so we can understand just how horrible it really was. Eleven thousand years ago was the last major earth axis shift and it quick froze mammoths eating in a field in Siberia when, all of a sudden, the landscape was almost immediately turned into a polar region where everything was dead. The Bible talks about this as being the destruction of the planet Rahab and other texts tell us 1/3 of the entire population of the earth was wiped out. A thousand years later another event temporarily shifted the earth melting the ice caps, forming massive tidal waves and drowning just about everything and everyone left on the earth. When the clamor had ended the earth shifted back to its 10 thousand year alignment as captured in the mid-Atlantic magma and the Hawaiian hot spot trail and life began again. This last event would be called the Pleistocene Extinction. While all this was going on, animals would die and on special occasions, they would fossilize. For decades, scientists have been using fossilization comparisons to date things, but there were problems. One was they kept finding giant people who lived with the dinosaurs. As the dinosaurs would walk along the beaches of that day, people would come one the same beaches. We believe they went to the beach at separate times, but both sets of footprints were fossilized together, most likely before the great extinction that ended the Cretaceous Period. I know all this seems bizarre right now, but it is important to understand just how unstable everything is and how the nuclear decay timing could get so messed up and how monkeys and apes were unclean because they were man-made.

Era/Period/Epoch	time (T yrs ago)
Archaeozoic period	50,000-3000
Proterozoic period	3000-1000
Cambrian period	1000-900
Ordovician period	900-800
Silurian period	800-700
Devonian period	700-600
Carboniferous period	600-500
Permian period [1st Mars event]	500-400
Triassic period [Mars Encounter]	400-300
Jurassic period [Titan]	300-200
Cretaceous period [ANAK]	200-100
Tertiary period [Cro-Magnon]	100-40
Pleistocene period [Flood]	40-10
Holocene period [Present]	10-0

Ape DNA

With the knowledge that people have been here for a long, long time, let's look at a very strange and curious discovery.

Ape DNA looks weird and they cannot find a common ancestor for the apes.

Much controversy has been evident today concerning apes and man. It seems that by DNA analysis the Chimpanzee and Bonobo must have come into existence after humans. I know that doesn't fit into our neat little world of evolution and survival of the fittest and it may even give concern to us about who should control the world. Those questions and concerns will be answered in good time, but before we can begin to re-establish a method to the madness known as evolution, we must first get better acquainted with the concept. Not only should our understanding be determined by scientific study and conjecture, but also by religious history and cultural legacy. Some may not like bringing in all three of these venues together, but if we don't, then I guarantee we will never have an answer that is remotely close to the truth.

Chromosomes

As creatures evolve, increasing the genetic information contained in chromosomes enhances species. This would be easily seen as an increase in chromosome packets; or so it would seem if there was anything to evolution enhancement or uncontrolled evolution in general. Below is a short list of common animal types. Beside each animal type is the number of chromosomes used as the building instructions. Notice that "Man" is much more highly evolved than most of the animals as it has more instructions. Wow! The theory works. Man is better than other animals because it is more highly evolved.

Virus	1	Ant	2
Parasitic roundworm	2	Indian deer	6
Fruit fly	8	Mustard	10
Microscopic roundworm	12	Rye	14
Guinea Pig	16	Dove	16
Corn	20	Horsetail plant	21
Opossum	22	Kidney bean	22
Redwood tree	22	Chinese deer	23
Earthworm	32	Yeast	32
Frog	36	Pig	40
Mouse	40	Wheat	42
Bat	44	**Man**	**46**
Tobacco	48	Apes	47
Sheep	54	Domestic Horse	64
Wild Horse	66	Dog	78
Chicken	78	Carp	104
Crayfish	200	Fern	500
Butterfly	380		

Split Chromosome

Another thing that should be brought up here is that Apes sort of have more Chromosomes that humans do. What I mean by that is that they have 47 and we have 46. Oh! No! It seems that we have de-evolved from the Apes by this logic. Apes, however, have one more pair of chromosomes because two sets of pairs; those called 2p and 2q, are put together to make a single chromosome pair in the humans, so the theory still holds as our DNA information is actually more compact in humans than in apes.

Inverted Chromosome

Still another thing that should be noted here is that almost all of the chromosomes are identical when comparing human and ape sets, so we possibly evolved from them. The only chromosome packets that differ are the 4th and 17th set. These two also are almost identical, but appear to be inverted such that the sequencing is the same but split in the middle and recombined in reverse order. So an ape is simply an "accidentally backward human" or the reverse with a man being an "accidentally backward Ape". It looks so strange someone might think that a human chromosome was purposely cut and reversed to form the ape. With all this weirdness, let's look at the 4 possibilities of developments.

DNA Similarity

Today everyone in biology can test analyze and give you information about mutations and similarities of DNA. When checking Chimpanzee they found there is about 1.5% difference in DNA. When checking Bonobo DNA, we find about 1.5% differences. Here is a strange part. The Bonobo and Chimpanzee have about 1.5% difference to each other and they are different differences. When checking their closes primate cousins [gorilla] we find something even more strange Chimpanzee and Bonobo both have about 3.5% difference when compared to gorilla DNA. That and the detail I presented earlier, Chimpanzee have fewer mutations occurrences than humans, there can be little doubt that Chimps came form humans. The separation of man and chimp has been estimated at many different dates. One DNA researcher timed the separation around 6000 years ago. I time it about 5500 years ago and we will get to that later.

Four Views Of Evolution

How did the ape come about? Let's say for a minute that you are somewhat skeptical that a highly advanced group of people lived with the dinosaurs and injected things into animal DNA to change the characteristics and even design APES. Therefore let's look at the 4 ways to evolve animals. In the area of evolution, these four distinct groups are vying for acceptance. Each has its own evolution determinant. Here are the 4 major concepts being presented today.

1. **Survival of the fittest** and uncontrolled evolution [This goes completely against the law of Entropy. While this really is problematic, it is still taught in some institutions. Also the beginnings are extremely problematic as the chemical groupings of DNA when randomized fall apart completely and the idea that enough identical strings of DNA could be altered simultaneously so that a colony of anything could be established is way out there. With new timing, this whole survival of the fittest thing has no time to react.]

2. **A master creator placed animal** strains with minor evolution of the original species. [For this to be accepted one must believe this great God made many mistakes in his designs which goes against the concept of an almighty creator.]

3. **Controlled Evolution**-Here I'm talking about ancient scientists changing characteristics in laboratories without total knowledge about what the outcome might be. [As they were just playing around with DNA like we do today, many mistakes occurred. The problem is there is no beginning in this one and the concept of DNA being life is not a correct one DNA is simply a group of sugars in a molecule. It is not alive. A dead DNA and a live DNA are identical.]

4. **The combination of 2 & 3** with a master creator making the original species and scientists manipulating the genetic codes to make "better" creatures. Unfortunately, the attempts would not always be for the best.

I don't want to influence your feelings concerning which one you believe except to say that ideas 1, 2, and 3 cannot work and design an Ape. OK number one could work, but there are flaws in the concept that need to be brought up. Let me give you some overviews that may begin to show you problems in each of the concepts.

Uncontrolled Evolution

Number one is the one we always here about in our schools. Here is the "Survival of the Fittest" Evolution Theory in a nutshell.

The Amoeba-There was a long time where no animals were here, but some chemicals randomly combined and simple animals like amoebas began to appear.

- Some of these amoebas mutated and became new creatures because there was ample time.
- The new creature was more complex than the first and mutated again and again each time getting more complex.

[By the way; this is totally against the LAW of ENTROPY as things should be trying to obtain lowest states and insure most randomness.]

These more complex creatures didn't make them more viable and put more stress on the environment. Today the true leaders in the environmental survival world are the single cell animals that have been here for millions of years. The amoeba has not had any mutated characteristic noted over the hundreds of years that it has been studied and it appears to be identical to those found millions of years ago. *[The question you might ask is, "If there was some innate reason for the amoebas to mutate and make it more viable, then why are they still around?"]*

Sex-Soon one of the mutations caused normal cell division to be an inappropriate method to reproduce and males and females appeared. One of the funny things is that almost identical mutations must have occurred at almost identical locations so that the two "identically mutated" animals could mate. In fact there had to be a significant group that converted simultaneously for this unbelievable action to occur or the offspring would not have creatures to mate with.

Advancement-The typical picture of evolution is that advancement occurs from this mutation, but that is not what occurs in the real world. In our controlled environments of today we find that most mutations degrade a species while very few if any enhance it.

The more reasonable model is that mutation controlled evolution is regressive.

In addition to that discussion will be elements of proof concerning the high probability of extensive genetic manipulation in the olden days. When I say olden days here, I mean many, many thousands of years ago. If we make statements about animal genetic manipulation, certainly we are disavowing the theory of evolution as it is stated today. When viewing evidence of our past, Darwin's Theory doesn't make sense. Even though it is wrought with problems, it is continually taught to our children. One of the reasons for this unfortunate thing is that it uses a central basis of fact surrounded by absurdities that are easier to accept than the alternative that is supported by the evidence. Scientists have found traces of less complex creatures that lived millions of years ago and by a process of common sense there must have been an evolutionary process to go from those first beginnings of life-forms to our present, advanced, super, all knowing one.

Spontaneous Life-Number two is the one we always hear about in our Churches. Here is the Spontaneous Life Theory in a nutshell. *God created every creature* the way he wanted them to be—no mistakes—no changes required. [even though the book of "Jasher" indicates that only 22 types of animals were created during the 6th Age]

Then God decided that some of the animals that he made were clean and others were abominable. God told Noah about the few that were acceptable and those that were abominations to him even before the worldwide flood. The list of unclean, detested animals included the ones you would expect to be horrible they include:

- **Dolphins, Whales,** and anything living in the sea without scales
- **apes and monkeys**
- **Eagles** and other majestic birds,
- **and the pig**, an animal with one of the largest brain to body size ratios, along with many, many others that, at first seem to make no sense.

While God supposedly created all animals in one day, many didn't appear for thousands or millions of years from the beginning according to DNA analysis tested against dozens of timing methods.

God placed vestigial legs and arms on whales and snakes, even though they never had real legs. It makes no sense that he would have created them with the useless parts.

He also put appendixes in humans even though there was no use for them.

He made flying creatures that couldn't fly, sea creatures that can live on the land, and land creatures that squirt blood out of their eyes. While most of these things seem to be mistakes, the theory won't let them be mistakes as God cannot make mistakes.

Let me say I don't believe that God makes mistakes so I will continue and he would not consider most of his animal creations as ABOMINATIONS. The Ape was not an abomination in how it acts and reacts to the world. God considered it an abomination for some other reason.

Genetic Engineering-Number three has possibilities and problems. Many of the planet seeding scientists seemed to try to get this one to work. In their theories, some highly advanced race from outer space seeded the earth. Here is the Genetic Engineering Theory in a nutshell.

- **Super humans came** from some other place.
- **Upon coming to the Earth** they began changing the environment and the animals that existed. They genetically modified animals and also used sexual relations to establish a huge environment of different creature types.
- **Once this was accomplished**, they left and evolution took control.

Hold on---If the scientists came from somewhere else, how did they get to where they came from?

Creator Initiated Genetic Enhancement-Number four is the one I like the best. It uses the best parts of two and three to build a useable environmental structure that could have been the backdrop for our existence today and it greatly reduces the anomalous artifacts and evidence that we have witnessed or dug up over the years.

- **God made humans** hundreds of thousands of years ago. These humans advanced their civilizations over many thousands of years.
- **Soon they were able to accomplish genetic** manipulation very similar to that practiced today.
- **They may have lived on earth** or somewhere else. It really doesn't matter.
- **Upon coming to the Earth** they began changing the environment and the animals that God had created. They genetically modified animals and also used sexual relations to establish a huge environment of different creature types.
- **Once this was accomplished**, they left, died off, or are still here and a level of evolution took control.
- **Periodically the earth** would go through a catastrophe that destroyed almost all life.
- **The genetic maps** [DNA of the various animals] had been stored somewhere and almost immediately following one of the catastrophes various forms of life could be reestablished quickly by ingenious genetic engineers.
- **Even after the last great catastrophe** "a worldwide flood", the genetic codes were pulled back out and a huge

variety of animals again were almost instantly, within a few thousand years, roaming our planet.

If you like one of the other theories and not the last overview that's fine, but before you completely shut out all possibilities of the others, let's look at the evidence. I'll start with scientific discoveries and show how they reveal different elements of the evolution of mankind. Then I will discuss the Religious aspects. While some may gain comfort in this section, many might not agree with what our most sacred references say about this subject. Finally I will combine cultural histories that may also provide some more details. Hopefully, this strange separation of data might be just what it takes to allow you to see a clearer picture unobstructed by religious and scientific bias. Once the pressure of common knowledge is stripped away, the obvious data and evidence can be finally viewed appropriately and you will see where the ape came from and where chimpanzee and a group called Vanara came from.

We are all used to seeing the standard evolution direction of mankind [as shown below] and believed that the ape evolution was similar. The problem is that any anomalous character that showed up as a fossilized anything was simply disregarded to protect the model. To me that is not science, that is criminal. Please understand something important. Neanderthal humans had a larger brain than modern humans.

Man Evolved

I've already talked about these ancient humans that lived with the dinosaurs and you can't find our ancestors on the graph because they would have raised questions. "If scientists can't even determine where people came from, how in the world can they tell where chimpanzees came from?" I always say. As we get back to the story, the ancient humans somehow survived to some level after the Heaven Wars that occurred at the end of the Cretaceous Era [120 thousand years ago]. The outcome of the war was that the rebels who had once been Homo-Gigantus were turned back into normal giant humans; the earth and heaven had been almost destroyed; the earth rotation began to slow down making everything on the planet heavier; and the result of the heaviness was that the really huge animals created generally became extinct.

Not the Rats-I know you were told that rats ate the dinosaur eggs and that killed the dinosaurs, but that is pretty silly. If you were a rat would you eat a dinosaur egg or a chicken egg? Many would choose the animal that could not turn me into mud, but somehow the chickens survived and the huge dinosaurs died. Either dinosaur eggs were really, really good, or the people making up the theories were trying to pull a fast one on you. Anyway, let me get back to the ape study. Some of the apes had already been designed before the fateful day that ended the Cretaceous Age, but we can believe that most died during the catastrophic event. Then they reemerged. Apparently, the losers of the war were turned into humans, but they still remembered exactly how to create many of the ABOMINATION animals including the Apes.

Speaking of Abominations-The evolution theories had issues, but when the new ape was discovered, it completely fell apart. Check out this set of prints below. Why does this ape seem to have such a horrible look on its face? The reason is obvious to a casual observer, but hard to accept by the ardent evolutionist, because, the fear experienced by this mammal was the fear of being eaten by an allosaurus long before it could have become evolved to the high form of the ape. The find was in upper New Mexico, but typically you don't see these things in textbooks.

No! These pictures were not produced with trick photography. The trick is trying to continue to accept evolution with all these Homo-Gigantus and Anak people around.

Normal Evolution Studies

Forget the allosaurus eating an ape. That simply can't happen, after all. On the flowing collage are some skulls of the most well-known hominids as we move from ape-like to man-like [left to right top to bottom] starting [with our new timing] 100 Thousand years ago with the Proconsul. Ramapithicus followed 95 thousand years ago; then Australopithecus 85 thousand years ago; Homo Habilis 80 thousand years ago; Homo Erectus 75 thousand years ago; Homo Sapien Neanderthalis 60 thousand years ago; and finally Homo-Sapien-Sapien/Cro-Magnon 40 thousand years ago. Proconsul was supposedly the evolutionary kernel of the apes. If you add in the fact that Homo-Sapien HUMANS were originally on the earth over 150 thousand years ago and walked with dinosaurs, you can see how the whole ape-seed thing might have a different beginning.

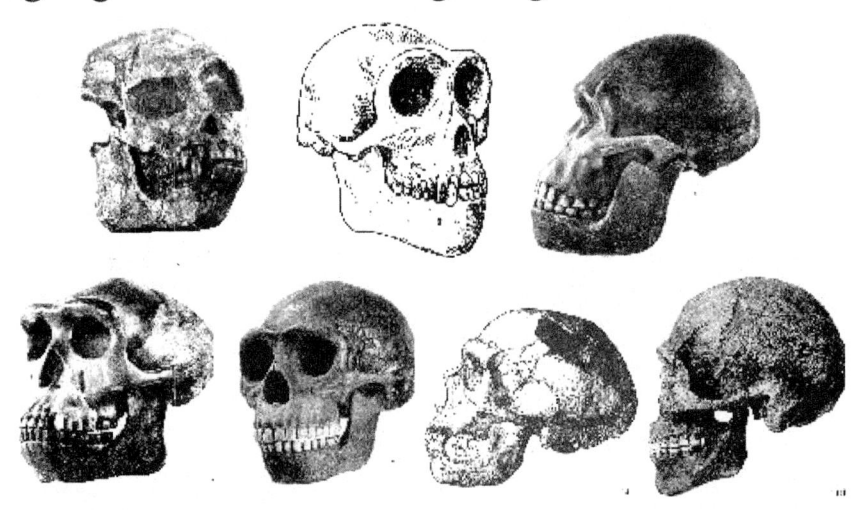

What the evidence tells us is that most of the different "Human" types and animal types were actually **experiments** as the Nephilim [the losers of the Heaven War] were trying to get the perfect human servant. The monkeys and apes may have simply been mistakes in their experiments.

Multidrop-Some scientists now believe that the Homo habilis is such an oddball that I wasn't even in line at all with modern humans while Heidelberg and Floresienesis continued the Habilis lineage. Instead, they now believe that Cro-Magnon might have been a completely different species while Oreopithicus turned into Robustus, Australopithecus, which tuned into Gigantopithecus [a 10 foot ape-man] followed by the Meganthropus which eventually became the Apes. The general chart is shown next.

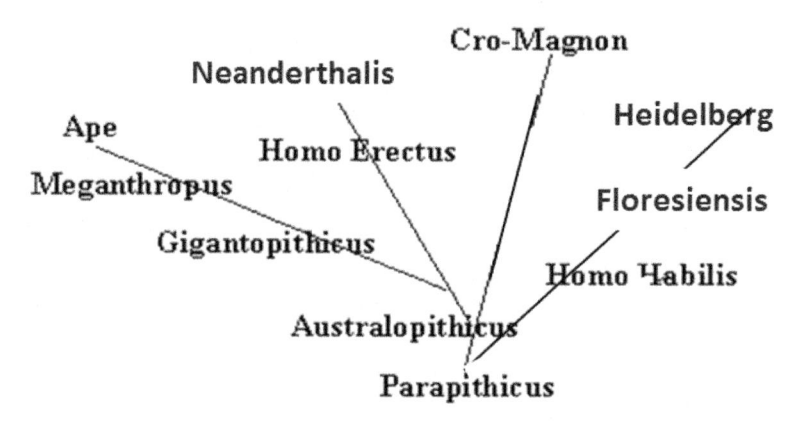

```
                    Cro-Magnon
          Neanderthalis
                                    Heidelberg
  Ape
              Homo Erectus
  Meganthropus
                                    Floresiensis
       Gigantopithicus
                              Homo Habilis
              Australopithicus
                  Parapithicus
```

If this doesn't look odd, when we add in the monkeys it goes nuts. It seems that nothing is associated with any other creature. Note how the monkeys and all apes are completely separate and how apes you would think would have a common union have essentially no union except for in some bleak time period in our distant past that is so far that you can say just about anything. Everyone is afraid to place any closer relationships to the apes because they are so vastly different. Let me tell you why that is. The Apes are experimental animals using human DNA splicing a hundred thousand years ago. Up until just before the worldwide flood. Notice in the following chart that all the expansion of manlike hominids is considered to be so similar that it is a single line. Please don't believe that this could have been done by some random mutation of chromosomes in some pit of oil. It seems that nothing has a similarity except to humans, because humans made them. The ancient humans not only wanted to just play with DNA for the fun of it, they were also looking for a servant.

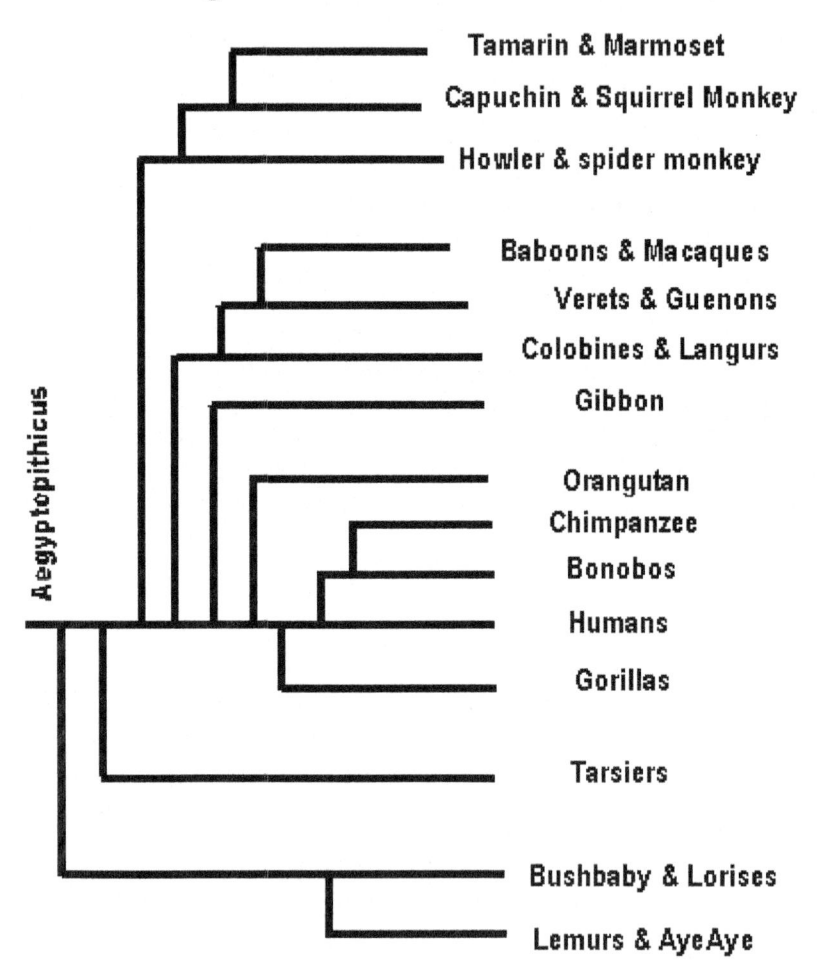

```
Aegyptopithicus ─┬─────┬──────────── Tamarin & Marmoset
                 │     └──────────── Capuchin & Squirrel Monkey
                 │     ────────────── Howler & spider monkey
                 │
                 ├─┬──────────────── Baboons & Macaques
                 │ ├──────────────── Verets & Guenons
                 │ └──────────────── Colobines & Langurs
                 │
                 ├───────────────── Gibbon
                 │
                 ├───────────────── Orangutan
                 ├─┬─────────────── Chimpanzee
                 │ ├─────────────── Bonobos
                 │ └─────────────── Humans
                 ├───────────────── Gorillas
                 │
                 ├───────────────── Tarsiers
                 │
                 └─┬─────────────── Bushbaby & Lorises
                   └─────────────── Lemurs & AyeAye
```

Search for a Servant

If we add in the ancient humans into the mix, we get something that looks a little different.

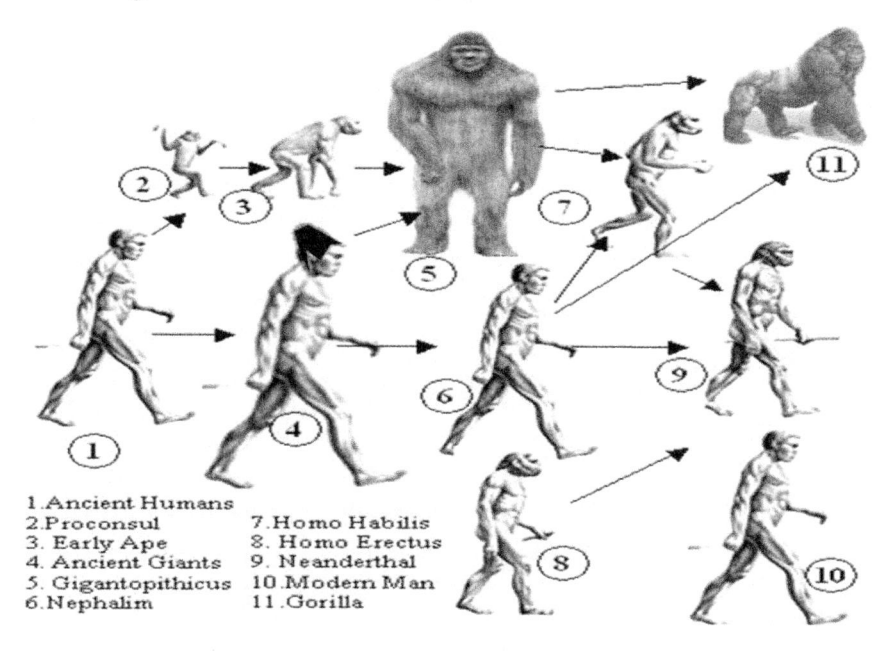

1. Ancient Humans
2. Proconsul
3. Early Ape
4. Ancient Giants
5. Gigantopithicus
6. Nephalim
7. Homo Habilis
8. Homo Erectus
9. Neanderthal
10. Modern Man
11. Gorilla

First thing you should see is that man has had no change. Number one and number 10 humans would look very close to the same over a period of over 150 thousand years. Just like the amoeba and all the other seemingly stationarily positioned species like the shark, clam, turtle, many plants, and many, many other animals of today. If we look at the ape, we find something entirely different.

45

Gibbon   Orangutan   Chimpanzee   Gorilla   Man

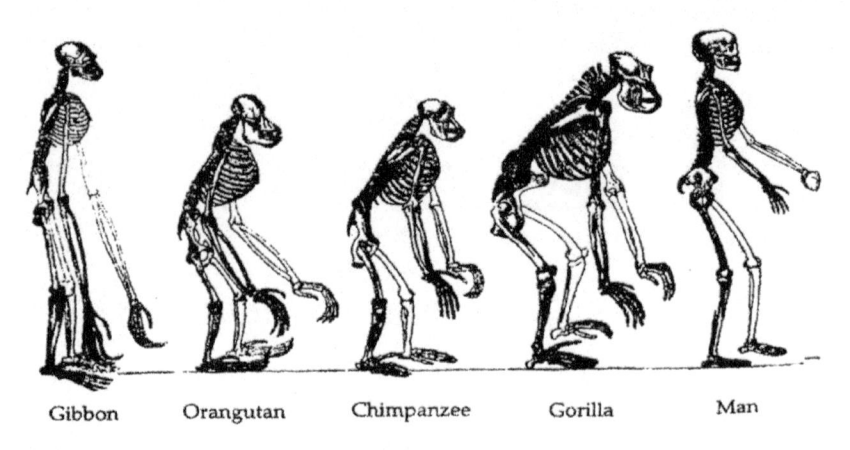

They all have drastic changes. Man isn't the end of the line for apes, He is the kernel used to design these things.

Genetics Designed Servant

Many texts tell us that the main reason the Anak people [also known as Nephilim] and the other humans were miserable was that they had to do **WORK**! It was no fun doing all the work; even if some of the work was to create monsters and different beings and other fun things. These Nephilim felt that they needed to make a new "man" to do the work and worship them as gods, but they were not having much success because the beings they made could not be domesticated. Why should they have to do work anyway? We find that many texts say the same thing. God felt compassion for the people and created them a worker-man. Let's look at an overview of stories relating to the creation of this new man from around the world before turning to the Mediterranean area and looking for Biblical similarity and enhancements. See how very similar the creation stories are even with the vast separation between people of the ancient times. Surviving writings are not as prevalent in the Americas, so the details and comparisons are somewhat limited. Even with the writing scarcity the American stories are the same as those found from the Middle East and other places, as we will see. Some of the details may not make too much sense right now but they will as later descriptions paint a pretty complete picture of not only the sixth-AGE creation, but also the things that followed. This collection comes from South America, Central America, North America, The Far East, Africa, and the Middle East. Not too many places have been left out, so how can we leave this timeline out of our "Normal History" classes? Here are some things to look for.

God Remade Man

The new man was still very primitive and many times depicted as **hairy or monkey-like**. While the Nephilim wanted them to, the new man would not worship god. The experimentation did not stop. The new man mixed with the Nephilim and the hair fell off and the man became smarter. [We will call this less hairy man Neanderthal.] Let me tell you something you probably didn't know about Neanderthal. From DNA samples we now know he was light sizing color and had red hair. When he talked, we now believe he had a high pitched nasally voice and knew about 80 words or so. Don't ask me how they know all those details. I simply don't know but I do know our image of Neanderthal is changing as his brain was larger than our current "atrophied" brain.

Historians Described the Experiment

Around the world the ancient historians wrote the same thing. Some were a little flowery in their descriptions, but the descriptions can be pulled out fairly easily. I have put a number of these texts following to show how widespread the knowledge of ancient genetics. While I didn't put the Book of Giants and Book of Secrets in this section, I will tell you that they also specifically indicate that genetics including the manufacture of abominable animals like the ape were carried on for centuries.

Man's Beginnings

Incan History of Man

This comes from Peru and the Inca. The time line of this history has been slightly changed because it was a little backwards from all others and was believed to have been "copied" in an incorrect order. According to several historians, I have put in the more correct time-line to limit confusion.

After a massive flood, Viracocha descended to the Earth and shaped animals. [After the Earth became without form and void from a huge Heaven-earth war, Viracocha and other Anak people, remade animals.]

"The god" re-made man. This time he endowed each man with his own language and brought him to life with his divine breath. [This is the story of the creation of man during the 6th "age". Notice that this was considered the RE-Make of man by "The God"]

He sent the giants among primitive man [Anak or other humans inbred with this primitive man. If forgot to tell you the Titans and Anak were giants]

Giant tunnels were built by the ancient race of white men to protect them from endless cataclysms [We now know that underground living was common around the world because of bomb blasting type wars that were fought over thousands of years. This will not be investigated in this book.]

The sons and daughters of the sun instructed them in a manner of knowledge including-language, customs, and art [Like almost all ancient texts, Angels and Nephilim taught normal humans everything.]

Viracocha and his disciples could walk on water. [Levitation was known and was similar to that described in the Bible as both Peter and Jesus walked over the water.]

Another great flood was sent to destroy the giants. All perished except one man and one woman. [The Noah story and the worldwide flood]

"After people arrived at Tulan and before going west, our language was the same. Our speech became different—alas we have abandoned our speech." [I know this sounds like the "Tower of Babel Story". I this case the city of Babel was called Tulan, but the rest is the same.]

Viracocha flew some of the people to other parts of the world. [In the Middle Eastern "Tower of Babel Story" mankind was also scattered over the world.]

Mayan History of Man

This section comes From "Popul Vuh [Book of Counsel]" or the Mayan Holy Book. I'm sure you will see a similarity.

After many wars and fighting, God separated the sky and the Earth, [Like hundreds of ancient accounts, the Earth split in two during the wars.]

Then the gods made trees [Trees were reintroduced before animals.]

Then animals were made, but the animals did not praise them. [Of course God didn't care about a goat praising him. This would have been talking about ancient humans that would have been part human like the apes and early ape-humans.]

The gods fashioned humans in hopes that they would worship them, but they were made out of mud and dissolved. [From this and hundreds of other texts we can determine that ape-man or Homo-Habilis was designed but he would not serve the Nephilimic humans.]

Then "He" made more humans out of wood. They looked like real people, but did not praise god because they had no memory and learned too much [This new human was created by God and he looked different than the earlier beings, including the Homo-Habilis. They were much more like the Nephilim. They were humans. This possibly would have been the Homo-Erectus.]

An imposter named Vukub-Cakix and his giant sons challenged the Gods [We will find that there is substantial concurrence of another attempt by Satan to take over heaven a long time after the first devastating heaven wars.]

God wreaked revenge by turning the world upside down. [There is no direct mention of this in our Bible, but geologic history shows that the Earth axis flips frequently, just as I indicated previously.]

Then God re-made man from maize. [Now we get to the time that Adam was created as true third true human.]

This time he limited man's understanding of the world. They finally praised God and light spread over the world. [God told man to stay away from the tree of knowledge.]

Aztec History of Man

This comes from their sacred book entitled "Five Creations of Man". Again the similarity is remarkable.

In the first creation giants walked the Earth. [Giant humans/Titans were created before a later man.]

After a battle, the giants were knocked into the water and the Earth was consumed by jaguars [After the war between heaven and the angels, the rebel angels were banished to Earth according to Jewish historical records.]

In the Second creation, the leader of the giants had another battle and took control. [A second attempt at taking over heaven was unsuccessful.]

During the second creation, people turn into monkeys and the world was destroyed by wind. [This seems to be saying that the Nephilim inbred with primitive ape-man.]

In the third period, the world was governed by the rain god and destroyed by a fiery rain sent by the creator. [We now know that there was a huge "fiery rain of meteors" that occurred about 13 thousand years ago and that 1/3 of the world's population was destroyed according to Biblical texts and other writings.]

In the fourth creation, the world was ruled by the water goddess. It was ended by a great flood and everyone turned into fishes- [Adam was finally created and then the great flood covered the world.]

In the fifth creation, God remade man, but the Earth remained in darkness until the sun was recreated.[

Sumerian Story

According to "The Epic of Creation (Enuma Elish)" and "Epic of Gilgamesh", the Sumerians tell about the same story as the Hittites.

Anshar, Anu, and Ashur were the first Trinity of God and controlled heaven before the second trinity was fathered by them. [**Anus from the Hittites and Anu are similar portions of the Godhead.**]

Ea /Enki, Enlil, and Marduk were the second God trinity and controlled heaven and Earth after the first trinity. [**El from Jewish history and Ea are similar portions of the Godhead**]

The first children of the gods were the Lahmu - 'the hairy ones'. [**This is probably talking about the first creation of man and seems to indicate that when they were first created they were like ape-men or maybe they were just hairy.**]

The Igigi, under the direction of Taimat rebelled against Enlil, and surrounded heaven. [**This is the Heaven War** *discussed previously with Taimat taking the Satan position.]*

One of the gods, Hubur, created a horned serpent, a mushussu-dragon, a lahmu-hero, an ugallu-demon, a scorpion-man, umu-demons, a fish-man, a bull-man, and others to fight in the war. **[Everyone said the same thing. Many monsters besides the Dragon were created especially for the Heaven War. The bull-man was like the Minotaur from Greek Mythology and like the half bull half man of the Hittite history.]**

Taimat made the dragon to be as a god to fight in the war. **[The dragon was not just another pretty face, but was so powerful, he was like a god. We will find this identical reference in the Jewish accounts.]**

Marduk destroyed Taimat in the heaven war. **[Clearly this is the same heaven war that is presented in Jewish history.]**

Aruru on the direction of Ea, mixed clay with the blood of one of the other gods to make seven men and seven women to bear the workload of the Igigi. **[This indicates that the 6th time period man was created by an ancient race under the direction of God. It also indicates that the human creation was to be a worker for the Igigi, another name for the ancient humans.]**

Later, under the direction of Marduk, mankind was created. **[This shows that a third human was created. The Bible called this guy Adam. We call him Cro-Magnon.]**

Enlil released several disasters upon man in sequence including disease, flood, drought, and the great flood. **[Many destruction periods were experienced before the flood. The Hittite text told of some and other works tell of others. The main thing is that the story has consistency.]**

Ea - advised mankind that listening to other gods would do them harm **[In the Biblical version God warned Adam not to partake of the Tree-of-knowledge.**

Adapa is created and given understanding, to teach mankind. **[Adapa, the Biblical Adam, was given wisdom by God to help the "other" humans on the earth.]**

Ea advises Adapa not to eat the bread of eternal life lest he forfeit his life on Earth. **[Most have heard of the tree of life. This is simple the bread version.]**

Ea advises Atrahasis to build a boat in which to weather the flood that would destroy the world. **[Most will recognize this as the Noah and the Arc story.]**

The Babylonian Update

The Babylonian version of the same story is called "Epic of Creation". It was written about 1200 BC, and it tells the same story again. My comments are in bold after each significant stanza. Again the timeline presented seems to be re-enforced.

When there was no heaven, no Earth, no height, no depth, no name, when Apsu was alone, **[God was in the beginning.]**

-When there were no gods- **[The angels were not at the beginning.]**

-In the waters, gods were created, **[Before gods/ancient humans were in heaven they lived on the earth.]**

Discord broke out among the gods although they were brothers, warring and jarring- heaven shook, **[This is the beginning of the "heaven war" discussion.]**

Apsu said, 'Their first-born children have manners that revolt me. Day and night we suffer. My will is to destroy them, **[This discussion of the first ancient humans having children.]**

Now the other gods had no rest, tormented by storms, they conspired [against heaven] in their secret hearts. **[In desperation, the ancient humans and angels decided to take over heaven as was discussed previously.]**

Taimat [same Taimat as the Sumerian history] said, "We will make monsters, and monsters and gods against gods will march into battle together." **[Like almost all the ancient texts, the leader of the rebellion began making beings to battle heaven.]**

[She made]-snarling dragons wearing their glory like gods. **[Of all the monsters, the Dragon was made above the rest and given the "Glory of the gods" which other texts simply call the "light".]**

Taimat plotted, she raged in turbulence and all have joined her, all those gods whom you begot, **[According to this Babylonian history, there may have been more than a 1/3 of the angels that revolted against heaven as indicated in Jewish histories.]**

Taimat has loosed the irresistible missile, chock-full of venom instead of blood, 'There is no pity in their weapons. **[The rebel leader made terrible weapons of destruction and used them against heaven.]**

All seven winds were created and released to savage the guts of Taimat, **[God uses his own weapons to defeat the rebels.]**

He smashed their weapons and tossed them into the net; the rebels found themselves inside the snare, they wept in holes and hid in corners suffering the wrath of god. **[God smashed the weapons of war and the rebels tried to hide.]**

He put in chains the eleven monsters, and all their murderous armament. **[Some of the beings were placed in chains just like the Jewish account.]**

When it was accomplished, the adversary was vanquished; the haughty enemy was humiliated; **[All the rebels were seized.]**

He split Taimat's body apart like a cockleshell; with the upper half he constructed the arc of sky, **[After the war God re-created the heavens.]**

He pulled down the bar and set a watch on the waters, so they should never escape. **[From other accounts we can be pretty sure this means that the loosing angels were turned into the Anak and they could never escape into heaven again.]**

He gave the moon the luster of a jewel; he gave him all the night **[God created the moonlit night.]**

Euphrates and Tigris rose from her eyes, **[God created new rivers.]**

Those gods who hung up their weapons defeated, whom he had scattered, **now fettered,** *he bound to his foot the eleven monstrous creations. He made likenesses of them all and now they stand at the gate of the abyss--* **[Hell [the abyss or hell] was made and many of the rebel angels were chained there.]**

Then Marduk, divided the gods: one host below and another above, three hundred above for the watchers of heaven, five times sixty for Earth, **[Three hundred of the Rebel Angels evidently repented and were forgiven. 300 were banished to Earth and became Nephilim.]**

When the Fifty Great Gods had sat down with the Seven who design the immutable nature of things, they raised up three hundred into heaven. **[Three hundred of the rebel angels were allowed back into heaven according to the Babylonians.]**

*Then the Anunnaki, the **erstwhile fallen**, opened their mouths to speak to Marduk: [**The Babylonians specifically indicated that the Anunnaki were the fallen angels {Nephilim} just like the Jewish historical records.**]*

*The Anunnaki said, "Let us build a temple. The Tall Babel Tower shall be built, as you desire. Bricks shall be set in molds and you shall name it "the Sanctuary". The Anunnaki gods took up the tools, one whole year long they set bricks in molds. By the second year they had raised it. It towered and was the symbol of infinite heaven. [**This story seems to be a substantially skewed Tower of Babel story, but at least the Babel name is similar to Jewish texts. For those not reading the previous book, the Tower and citadel in Jewish texts was built west of Shinar or in Lebanon and it was made with huge blocks with at least one is 1000 tons. The images below show some of the massive ruins. The tiny people are normal sized. As shown in the lower left the stones were so easy to position the really large ones weren't used until the 5th layer.**]*

*Blood to blood I join, blood to bone I join from an original thing, its name is MAN, aboriginal man is mine in making. They cut Kingu's [one of the Nephilim] arteries and from his blood they created man; and Ea imposed his servitude. Ea [God] had created man and man's burden. This thing was past comprehension. [**The creation of 6th time period man is just like in the Bible story.**]*

56

Black-headed men will adore him on Earth; the subjected shall remember their god. Let them serve the gods, work their lands, build their houses. Let black-headed men serve the gods on Earth He created man a living thing to labor forever, and gods go free, to make, to break, to love, and to save. For your relief he made mankind, it is in the mouth of black-headed men who remember him. **[This is talking about the 6th time period man being black. Like all the other ancient texts, this creation was made to serve the Nephilim. It should be noted that Homo erectus was found in Africa.]**

The seed, created races of men from the world's quarters. From the stuff of a fallen god she made mankind. **[From the seed of the original 6th time period man, other hybrid races were made around the world.]**

Zoroastrian Story

According to the "ZAND-AKASIH", part of the Zoroastrian Biblical Texts, we find a similar "creation story". Let's see what it had to say. In their story, Ahriman was Satan and God was called Ohrmazd. I have changed those names to allow easier reading and after the verses I have provided comments. The comments are just comments, but please look at the similarities between the various writings so that you can gain a better perspective of probable truth.

*Ohrimazd [**God**] was, forever, at the highest, in the Light. Ahriman [**Satan**] was, at the abysmal station, in darkness. Betwixt them was a Void.*

God made beings and for three thousand years, they remained in the spiritual state. **[I believe this may be saying that the first humans turned into spirits or angels.]**

God, first, produced the seven fundamental Beneficent Immortals. **[Just like the Biblical history 7 archangels were created first.]**

Of the material creations: first, the Sky, second, the Water, third, the Earth, fourth, the Tree, fifth, Beneficent Animal, sixth, the Man, **[The 6 time periods of creation are similar to the Biblical account.]**

Out of His own Self, out of the Essence of Light, God created forth the spirit body of his own beings. **[God's creation contained a spirit.]**

God created six heavens they are as follows: the first is the Cloud station, the second the Sphere of the constellations, the third the unmixable Stars, the fourth is around the Moon, the fifth is called Endless Light, the sixth the Throne of the Beneficent-Immortals, the seventh the Endless Light, the Throne of God. **[Only 6 heavens described, and only the last two seem to be spirit places.]**

During the fifth time, God created a cow and from it, he created 282 species of animals. He also created Gav **[probably a depiction of Lilith]**; she was white and shining like the Moon. **[This creation of human was before the Gayomard creation of man on the 6th time period.]**

During the 6th time, God created Gayomard. He was possessed of eyes, ears, tongue and a mark; the mark was that mankind was born of God's seed. From that seed, men came forth from the earth in the body of the plant rovas. **[The mark may be just a strange depiction of a soul and I don't know where the plant comes in, but you have the data.]**

He created Gayomard, with Gav out of the Earth. **[Man/Adam was created out of dust like all histories and Lilith/Gav was his first wife.]**

Satan miscreated beings and they became useless. God saw the defiled and bad beings, they did not delight Him. Satan's was downfall was the unrighteous creation of the beings and ignorance. *[**Satan and the soon to be rebel angels defiled God's beings with genetic manipulation.**]*

God said: "Satan! Offer praise, unto my beings." Satan spoke: "I shall offer praise; I will, rather, destroy thee and thy beings too, I will turn thy beings against Thee" *[**Satan and his companions rebel against God and would not worship man.**]*

Satan also miscreated Akoman, and the other Demons. *[**Satan made special beings. They were made to fight in the heaven wars.**]*

God saw that his creation was mixed with light and darkness. *[**The beings including humans were becoming hybrids part from the Anak/Satan and part from God's original creation.**]*

A military congress became manifest on Earth; as the "Armies of men" advanced together in battle array. *[**Once all the human creations were accomplished Heaven wars began.**]*

God stationed the "Armies of the holy". Satan did not find the way of retreat there from; he saw the destruction of the demons and his own inability. God saw His own final victory. *[**Satan and the rebels lost the war and became Nephilim/Anak people.**]*

*[**After the heaven war**,]* Satan was stupefied, for three thousand years; the demons waged war in the material world" *[**When the Nephilim were defeated in the Heaven War, they started fighting in the material world. We will see other evidence of the terrible wars.**]*

Satan, with all the demons, *[**again**]* rose against the Luminaries [angels]. The Firmament was in revolution; the Sun and the Moon were in motion towards the world. *[**Heaven War #2 was a common theme in many societies.**]*

Satan drew the Star station down towards the void he stood within one third; like a serpent. **[The Biblical history indicates that 1/3 of the angels followed Satan against God and that he was like a serpent.]**

For ninety days, the Spiritual Yazads were combating, in the material world, with Satan and all the demons, until they were thrown into hell defeated. **[By this we can believe that not only do the Nephilim rebels lose a second heaven war, but also, hell was not created until a long time after the first heaven war.]**

Gayomard spoke: "All mankind will be of my seed. **[Gayomard and Adam are apparently the same. He was the beginning of the Adamic/ Cro-Magnon humans.]**

Goshorun, came out of the body of the Gav. God spoke: "Thou art ill, Oh Goshorun; thou hast borne the illness from Satan **[Very similar to the Cain [Goshorun] story of the Bible.]**

Tibetan History

From "The Monkey and the Rock Ogres"-*The Ogres were a race of devils* [Anak people "followers of Satan" were on the Earth before "Adamic" man.]

One of the females became smitten with lust with a monkey. [The Anak experimented on the ape-man according to ancient Sumerian and other texts.]

The two were united as husband and wife and she bore 6 monkey children. [The Anak finally had children with ape-men & women. More than likely this was done artificially.]

Some of the children were misshapen, loathsome, stupid and vulgar. [This is identical to Greek mythology. Just imagine how many mistakes were enjoyed by the haphazard manipulation of DNA back in the good old days.]

Some of them were endowed with wisdom, patience, virtue and sensitivity. [This would have been the Neanderthal hybrid man designed just before God recreated humans a third time as the one called Adam.]

The children lived in the forest of Assembled Birds and they had insatiable appetites. [A reference to the giants eating everything around as referenced in the ancient Jewish *"Book of Giants".*]

After three years, they had eaten all of the food that was available and God sprinkled seed to fill the garden with crops that required no cultivation [The Garden of Eden]

The monkey-children' hair and tails grew shorter. They then learned to speak and became human. [Just like the Middle Eastern versions, the hybrids were no longer like apes.]

Another Tibetan Story

The Tibetan Book "Dzamba Lying" shows similarities with the other ancient historical works in reference to some of the topics, especially the idea that the rulers were giants.

In the beginning Dzamba Lying had no people, animals or plants. **[The earth had no life.]**

Then it was visited by beings from Rirab Lhunpo. **[Nephilimic Humanoids arrive.]**

The beings were gods and established themselves on earth. **[They became the rulers.]**

In the process they became human **[Just like other ancient stories, these gods bred with humans.]**

Then there was a period of war and turmoil. **[The Heaven Wars are talked about again.]**

Afterward they selected a king named Mang Kur. **[This must be the king of the 6th day/Nephilim hybrid human.]**

He taught building and agriculture. [**This hybrid was very intelligent.**]

Book of Dzyan Story

The "Book of Dzyan" is a collection of 9 Sanskrit tablets again from Tibet as these Tibet people must have really thought about where people came from. In them we find the descriptions of a total of 7 individual creations of humans over the years. Some of them were human, some were more spirit than human, but the information does go along with other data being presented. As with the other data, look for the similarities and conformance rather than the more outlandish elements as they could have been added as a matter of explanation of unknown elements of the writer. These, skewed remarks, should not detract from the information that can be obtained.

The Primordial Seven produced from their circumgyrating breaths the Fiery Whirlwind. [This is possibly talking about the beginnings of the solar system with 7 fiery whirlwind masses.]

Seven strides through the seven regions above, and the seven below. 7 heavens and 7 hells are alluded to [quite a few less than the normal 12.]

The swift son of the divine sons runs circular errands. He passes like lightning through the fiery clouds. He rebuilds them like the older wheels placing them on the imperishable centers [Sounds like a massive cometic planetoid that brings life and stabilizes the orbits in some way. The Sumerians may have called this planet Niberu, but the story is similar.]

At the fourth level [of heaven], the sons were told to create their images. One third refused & two thirds obeyed. A curse was pronounced; they will be born on the fourth, suffer and cause suffering. This is the first war. [This is not only describing the first heaven war, but also is discussing genetic breeding. Even the indication that 1/3 of the angels rebel is consistent with the Biblical version of this very ancient time in history.]

There were battles fought between the Creators and the Destroyers, and battles fought for space; the seed appearing and re-appearing continuously. [There have been many destruction periods on the earth. The seed re-appearing idea presented here seems to refer to re-establishment of animals after each successive destruction period by genetic replacement as I have presented earlier.]

They slew the forms that were two- and four-faced. They fought the goatmen [Satyrs], and the dog-headed men, and the men with fishes' bodies. [The outcome of the breeding was sometimes not good. The men with fish bodies are of particular interest as the Sumerians, Dogon, and Hindu all worshiped such a being.]

Seven times seven shadows of future men were born [seven races?], each of his own color and kind; each inferior to his father. [This seems to indicate that the Ancient humans were more advanced that the predecessor races. This is consistent with the evidence that has been found. Seven races might be as follows:* [Ancient humans, Nephilim, 6th Age humans, Nephadim, Monstrous offspring of the Nephadim, Adamic humans, and finally mixed humans.]

[First Race] The first were self-born from the brilliant bodies of the Lords, The first, on every zone, was moon-colored; [First creations were the Archangels and would most likely have radiant bodies.]

[Second Race] Their sons were the children of the Yellow Father and the White Mother. This Second Race was A-Sexual – They were yellow like gold; [The second creation was evidently, the Ancient humans.]

[Third Race] From the second evolved the Egg-born, the third. First male-female, then man and woman. The third remained mind-less. These were set apart among the Seven. They became narrow-headed. This third was red. The Third Race became the Vahan of the Lords of Wisdom. They begat upon them dumb Races. Dumb they were themselves. But their tongues untied. The tongues of their progeny remained still. [The third creation was the 6th day man. The idea of egg born may be referring to being genetically manufactured in an "egg" container.]

Events after the 6th day Man-The book of Dzyan may give us some insights into what may be following.

*The **Fourth Race** finally developed speech. The fourth brown, which became black with sin. They became tall with pride. We are the kings, it was said; we are the gods.* **They took wives** *fair to look upon. Wives from the mindless, the narrow-headed. They bred monsters. Wicked demons, male and female.* [The 4th creation was the Nephadim. Just like the history provided in the book of Enoch, and the Bible, these beings took human wives. Can you see a similarity to the previous discussion of Nephadim? The angels became prideful and black with sin and when they bred with humans, the offspring were monstrous.]

[Fifth Race] Monsters they bred. A race of crooked red-hair-covered monsters going on all fours. A dumb race to keep the shame untold. [The "Book of Giants" indicated that the offspring of the Nephadim were giants and MONSTERS.]

Then the time came to rid the Earth of these large beasts and, by spells and devices, a large heavenly stone crashed into the Earth and caused a long time of darkness and cold. Thus did the large, lumbering beings come to the end of their season. [A meteor hit the earth and it was followed by an Ice

Age. This discussion of giant heavenly stones is telling the same story as is held in the evidence.]

The first great block of water came and swallowed the great islands. "All" Holy were saved, the Unholy destroyed. [This is describing the worldwide flood that most of have heard of. It alludes to the fact that more people survived than the 8 indicated in the Bible.]

Chinese Description

The Chuang-Tzu text from China contains a great description of this hard working servant. He seemed to always have a smile no matter what type of workload he was given. You would think that the Nephilim would love this worker, but it continues to indicate that the new man would not speak to the Nephilim and not worship them.

They appeared to smile as if pleased. Absent-minded they kept forgetting speech. They behaved as though wanting in themselves, but without looking up to others [did not worship God] In that which was One [of God], they were of God; in that which was not One [of God], they were man. And so between man and the divine no conflict ensued. This was not to be a true man. [Like most of the ancient texts the man created on the 6th day/time period" Homo Erectus" was not the Adamic man "Cro-Magnon".]

Ngombe Tribe History of Man

First there were no men. People before men lived in the sky. [Strange-No men but the men that were here when they weren't here lived on planets. Where have we heard this before? Anyway these guys certainly thought very ancient people lived on the earth OR nearby.]

A magnificent Garden was made for man [Something like the Garden of Eden was made.]

A female saw a hairy man in the forest [Here we go with the Nephilim inbreeding with primitive man.]

She married him and removed his hair. [The hybrid man was created from the union. This could be the homo-habilis ape-man or they might be talking about the hybrid made from the homo-erectus man; Neanderthal.]

The evil Ebenga, a serpent god, tempted the woman [Does this sound like the Biblical "Eve tempted by the serpent" story?]

Afterwards, her child brought witchcraft and misery into the world [Cain is born as was described in the Genesis book of the Bible.]

Bantu History

The Creator made the world. Then he made man out of clay. [This, evidently, was the ancient man and the being made out of clay is a common theme.]

Man turned out to be a lizard. [Shock of shocks! This sounds like a primitive version of man before man designing lizards and dinosaurs.]

God put him in the ocean for 5 days. On the 6th day he was still a lizard [6th day man was created next but he was not completely like man of today.]

After getting back in the water, he became a man on the 8th day. [The eighth day man was Adam according to the Bible and the Bantu.]

Rhodesian Description

The stories from the Wahungwe tribe of Rhodesia seemed to infer that there was a continual genetic manipulation study going on with the 6th day man. After some time, the "man" could have offspring with Nephilim and the offspring evidently could procreate on their own and the Nephilim didn't have to continue to inbreed with the humans.

The first night Mwueti [probably Ape man?] touched Morongo [a Nephilim?].

Each night she gave birth to different animals [genetic manipulation].

Finally she had regular children [hybrid people].

After that Mwueti had sex with his daughters [The hybrid man was finally able to procreate] *and the human race was formed.*

Babylonian History

I'm just about through please stay with me as I try to show that the development of mankind was not a Middle Eastern made up story and everywhere in the world we find similar discussions. This one comes from a text called the "Atra Hasis" that was found along with the earlier Sumerian creation story reference in other sections.

When the gods instead of man did the work, they bore the loads. The gods' load was too great. The work was too hard. The trouble was too much. The great Anunnaki made the Igigi carry the workload sevenfold. [For those not knowing who the Anunnaki were, they were the same as the Jewish ANAK which was simply another name for the Nephilim. The Igigi were the angels. These Nephilimic humans had to do their own work before the 6th day man came along.]

Let the womb-goddess create offspring, and let man bear the load of the gods!" [The way the womb-goddess made new creations was by manipulation of the DNA. In this case, the Nephilim took Homo Erectus and made the Nephilim, I think. We know the rest.]

Biblical History

I'm sorry I had to bring you through all the different civilizations of the world, but it important for you to know that it is not just Judeo-Christian historical references that help us here. While I already discussed the Genesis 1 confirmation of the genetic manipulation and creation of the 6th day human, there are other verses we should look at as well.

Genesis 3 tells us that because Eve listened to the serpent that *"a woman's childbearing would be MORE painful that it was before"*. The problem with this statement is that Eve had never had any children. It must have been talking about Eve having more pain that the "Normal humans" or the verse doesn't make sense.

Genesis 6 tells us that *"Nephilim and giants lived before Adam and that angels fathered children. This entire group was the giants of old."* While Adam and his clan were not the offspring of angels and while the Bible would not reference "Giants" after Adam except for his clan, it is obvious that this references "Giants" living before Adam.

Let's look a little closer at the Re-made statement. [Man was re-made according to the Bible-Genesis 1:30]-The Bible is specific in telling that man was **re-made** to **re-plenish** the Earth again. Here are a few more examples from the Bible and associated documents that may amplify the Genesis statements and describe more about how man and apes were eventually designed.

Jewish Essene Text

Enoch II 30:8*-And during the 6th Age I commanded my wisdom to create man.* [It is strange that it specifies God's wisdom rather then he himself creating man during the 6th Age.]

Apostolic Constitution 7.34.6*-Having given order by your wisdom, you created, saying, "Let **US** make man according to **OUR** image and likeness."*

Jasher 4:16-18*- And all the sons of men taught one another their evil practices and they corrupted the Earth, and the Earth was filled with violence. And their rulers [**Nephilim**] went to the daughters of **men** and took [**this taking is sexual**] their wives by force from their husbands and the sons of men in those days took [**not sexual usually**] from the cattle of the Earth, the beasts of the field and the fowls of the air, and **taught the mixture of animals of one species with the other**, in order therewith to provoke the Lord; and God saw the whole Earth and it was corrupt, for all flesh had corrupted its ways upon Earth, all men and all animals.* [Corrupted animals did not mean the animals were evil, it meant that the species were changed inappropriately.]

Jubilees 5:2*- And lawlessness increased on the Earth and all flesh corrupted its way, alike men and cattle and beasts and birds and everything that walks the Earth all corrupted their ways and their orders.* [The only way that animals corrupted their way was that they were genetically manipulated and just weren't the same animals.]

Jubilees 7:24*- Afterwards **they sinned against beasts** and birds and everything that moves or walks upon the Earth.*

[There are two ways to sin against beasts- sex and genetic manipulation. God didn't like either.]

Enoch II 59:5-6- *But whosoever kills a beast without wounds, kills his own soul and defiles his flesh. And he who does any beast any injury whatsoever, in secret, it is evil practice, and he defiles his own soul.* [The killing and injury done in secret was not killing animals for food, it was the genetic manipulation and corruption by integrating mans; genetic material.]

Jewish Gnostic Text

Book of Abraham 4:27-"*And the* **gods** *said, let* **us** *go down and form man in our own image—and the gods said we will cause them to be fruitful and multiply and* **RE-plenish** *the Earth. We will give them life and they will be very obedient.*" [As I mentioned previously, the use of the word us cannot be considered reasonable for the Creator. Instead the first part of this verse may be talking about the Nephilim experimenting with animals to create the Homo-Habilis with the second part talking about the creation of the Homo-Erectus.]

"Hypostasis of the Archons"-*Come let us [rulers of the world] make a man that will be soil from the Earth. They modeled the being as wholly of the Earth. Now the rulers [also] made the body of a female with the face of a beast* [**genetic mistakes**].—*And he breathed into his face and the man came to have a soul and remained on the ground—the spirit saw the soul-endowed man upon the ground and the spirit descended and came to dwell within him and that man became a living soul.*

Naphtali 1:25-27- *The Gentiles went astray, and forsook the Lord and changed their order, and obeyed stocks and stones, spirits of deceit—become not as Sodom, which changed the order of nature. In like manner the watchers also changed the order of nature, whom the Lord cursed at the flood, on* *account he made the Earth without inhabitants and fruitless.* Not only does it indicate that the watchers or angels and gentiles [not pure Adamics] practiced genetic manipulation, but also that the practice was the major cause for the flood.]

Generation of Adam 6:1-5-*Among our little ones was Timnor and Ammah. Timnor understood physical law and created mighty machines. Ammah understood the secrets of creation. She manipulated the very fountain of life until she had created new forms of beings dedicated to the destruction of mankind* [As in other texts, manipulation of species was common practice and the results were not always helpful to man and were always against God. In this case, the verse is talking about the direct descendants of Adam manipulating animals.]

Iranian Text

Zadspram [Iran]- *From the seed which was the ox's, they would carry off from it and the brilliance was entrusted to the angel of the moon in a place that seed was thoroughly purified by the light and was restored in its many qualities.* [After the angels corrupted the animal genetic code, God had to recreate them.]

Jewish Historian Text

The Antiquity of the Jews-*"On the sixth day he created the four-footed beasts, and made them male and female: on the same day he also formed man."*

Modern Texts

Edger Cayce- According to the 20th century Seer, " *The original sin of man was, in fact,* **the misuse of the creative powers** *to satisfy the self."* [Making animals is a no no.]

Book Of Secrets

The "Book of Secrets" found among the Dead Sea Scrolls provides two things. First it gives us a backdrop of scientific experimentation without restraint and secondly it is a warning. It is a very strong warning about the use of secrets of God like genetic manipulation without regard for creation. The book simply says that if we use the secrets, the same thing will happen that happened before. The earth will be destroyed again. Not by him, but because we don't understand what we are doing as we manipulate "Nature". Of the secret elements indicated in the text, it seems that the "manipulation of creation" is the worst. This almost assuredly references the genetic manipulation, like making apes, and transmutation that was continuously employed by the rulers and humans before and immediately after the Pleistocene Extinction flood. Here are the major elements of what has been pieced together of the "Book of Secrets". Judge for yourself. The bracketed information is my commentary.

Those who would penetrate the origins of knowledge, along with those who hold fast to the wonderful mysteries (of magic;) [This is talking about humanoids known as gods and humans that practiced the secrets of "magic". What we find out is that those who partake in the "magic" are in trouble.]

--those who walk in simplicity as well as those who are devious in every activity of the deeds of humanity; those with a stiff neck, and all the mass of the Gentiles, [This warning is for all humanoids including those that were not pure blood Adamic humans were not left out of this warning.]

--with (this I beseech your attention. All of the) secrets of sin (and magic were known) but they **[preflood humanoids]** *did not know the secret of the way things are nor did they understand the things of old.* [No one knew the ramifications of meddling with nature before the flood.]

They did not know what would come upon them, so they did not rescue themselves without the secret of the way things are. [Magic did not warn or save any of the ancient societies from the flood.]

It is true that all the peoples reject evil, yet it advances in all of them. Who wants his money to be stolen by a wicked man, but where is the people that has not robbed the wealth of another? [No humanoid can escape evil. Even if he thinks that he is doing good, it can change to evil.]

What shall we call man who will call no one on earth wise or righteous? It is not a human possession (to act on wisdom.) It is not (possible because) wisdom is hidden except for the wisdom of cunning evil, and the schemes of Belial (who modified creation,) a thing that ought never to be done again, except by the command of his Maker. [Only God has the wisdom to modify creation. Belial (possibly a term for Satan) modified creation and it should NEVER be done again. This almost assuredly includes genetic manipulation, alchemy, and all the other magic areas. All of which we are doing today in somewhat minor ways.]

(God controls) every secret, and he limits every deed and what (magic that is known by) the Gentiles, for He created them and their deeds also [The magic that is done by the non-Adamic humanoids is only allowed by God. None is accomplished without his knowing.]

Consider the soothsayers, those teachers of sin and (magic. Do not regard) your foolishness, for the vision is sealed up from you, and you have not properly understood the eternal mysteries. [Manipulation of nature and Magic cannot be understood by man. It is foolish to try to use them for good.]

You have not become wise in understanding (my secrets); for you have not properly understood the origin of Wisdom. [In order to understand how to manipulate nature in a good way, you must understand how it came into being, which you cannot.]

"The Book of Giants"

Like the Book of Secrets, the Book of Giants is another Jewish Essene text found with the Dead Sea Scrolls. It confirms the art of genetic manipulation including development of apes, monsters, and the mess that occurred from it. The best way to describe what was in the "Book of Giants" is to present the portion that is still extant that pertains to genetic manipulation. You will see that God was certainly annoyed at the giants eating men, but according to this book and several other texts, the real kicker was the biological experimentation that the Giants did to the animals. We will never know the extent of their modification of species, but God hated it. Here is the "Book of Giants". After each verse is a short interpretation. [They are my interpretations, so take them for what they are worth.]

*For they [**a group of ancient ones called the Nephadim,**] knew the secrets of heaven and sin was great in the Earth because of their experiments. They made mistakes and they killed many animals and people. They had sex with women and they begat giants.*

These were bad Angels that somehow became human. Like other groups of humans, these people and their offspring experimented with genetics.

They selected two hundred donkeys, two hundred asses, two hundred rams of the flock, two hundred goats, and two hundred other beasts of the field.

The Nephadim performed unnatural acts, and begat giants and dragons.

From every animal, and from every type of human was taken its seed for mixed sex.

It strongly suggests that human and animal genes were mixed together.

After a time they defiled the animals and people and begot giants, monsters, and dragons. God saw all that they begot, and, behold, all the Earth was corrupted with their blood and by the hand of man. They were brought food which did not suffice for them and they turned on mankind.

If that wasn't bad enough, the giants started eating people.

They began to get hungry and they were seeking to devour many animals and people. The people ran to a safe place but the monsters and dragons attacked it. Man's flesh was eaten by all the giants. The monsters thought that they would be saved and they would arise after death, but it was not so because they were lacking in true knowledge of heaven and because they were abominations of the Earth.

The giants did not understand that they would not go to a heavenly place after death and I'm sure their parents told them about the marvels of this other world. Here is something, I think, needs to be stressed here. All of the hundreds of indications in the ancient texts about genetic manipulation were written before man had regained knowledge about this type of capability. How could they have the concept of a horse with a man's torso unless the results of the experimentation were seen or told about?

There you have it. Humans creating genetic variants were horribly dangerous; not only because the outcome was inappropriate, but also because they simply could not know the essence of life in general.

Aegyptopithecus

While there were many attempts at making human-like animals prior to this one, the one we mostly identify as the beginning of apes is the *Aegyptopithecus*. This simple ape like thing might have been the schematic for many of the apes we have today and the characteristics they generated were much more human that previous attempt.This *Aegyptopithecus* was supposedly the first of the apes and it lived near the beginning of the Tertiary period well after the ancient humans roamed the earth. It was a tiny thing with a brain size of about 22 CM^3. And, as you might expect, the frontal brain lobes are considered to be rather small in fact some indicate that it is not even primate like. It size was only about 7 kg and the length of its femur was about 150mm so we are talking about an insignificant animal that the ancient humans began experimenting with. If you still are stuck on the evolution thing, this is the evolutionary base of all primates. Its skull is shown below. I made it big so it would not seem so insignificant.

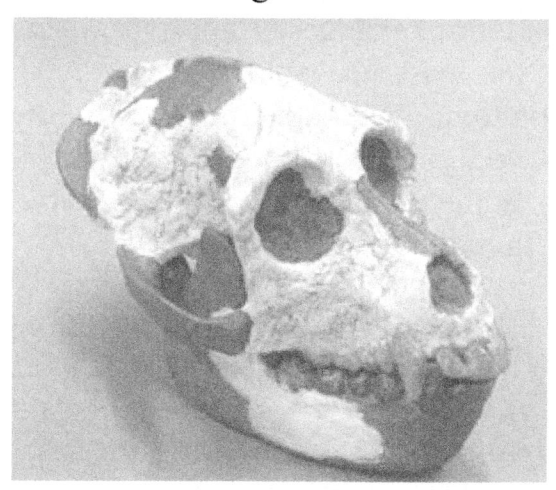

Australopithecus

Possibly the most famous of all of the Australopithecine humanoids is Lucy. The drawing to the left below shows what Lucy may have looked like when she was alive. Even though she could stand up like a tiny 3.5 foot female, she certainly was an ape. She was a little more advanced than proconsul but she was still not a human. If she put her arms down they would reach her knees. Civilized humans certainly existed during the time of the Australopithecines, like Lucy, but they were the ones in the white coats administering gene therapy on groups of the apes of the time. Lucy and the Australopithecine descendants ran around like lab rats, but the early people of this age used the entire world as their lab. Some of the Australopithecine genes were most likely used to seed new humanlike and new ape creations, but it was not done by random exchange, or survival of the fittest. Many times, it was the least survivable that survived, simply because the mutations was interesting to the geneticists of the day. Next right are some of the many skull types that were created. Some are apes some are quasi human, and some are very human looking.

That brings us up to the next advancement in "Human-like apes". This guy was called the Homo-Habilis.

Homo-Habilis

We can believe that the Homo Habilis was similar to Oliver. The Nephilim would have been so proud. "This new one even walks like us better than the last one and his brain is twice as big," they said to themselves. They may have even gotten an equivalent to the Nobel Peace Prize, if that was not just a presidential candidate prize at this very ancient time. Try as they might, the experiments were failures after this when they tried to make human servants and workers. All the Nephilim and other humans could do was to make monkeys and apes.

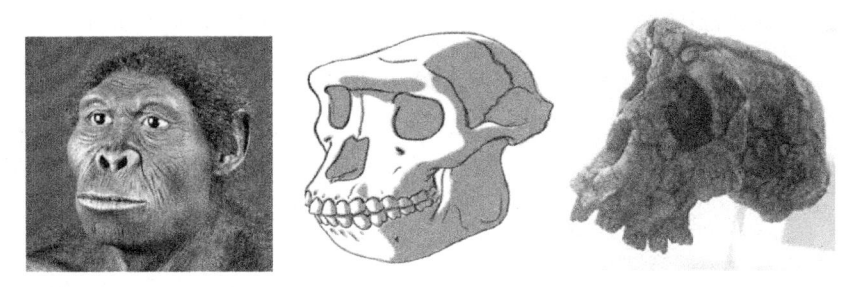

They injected their own DNA. They tried seminal transfer. They probably tried everything. They could not do any better. With a need to design workers to run the McDonald's of the day, we are told they cried out to the creator Go for help. We cannot make a McDonald's worker, they cried. Apes were everywhere, maybe even baboons, but none of them could help the humans. They had to make their own hamburgers. Below is one of the skulls of the Habilis. Note the heavy brow ridge, but smooth skull. This guy had an ape-like heavy jaw and not much of a nose, but there were differences between Habilis and the modern apes.

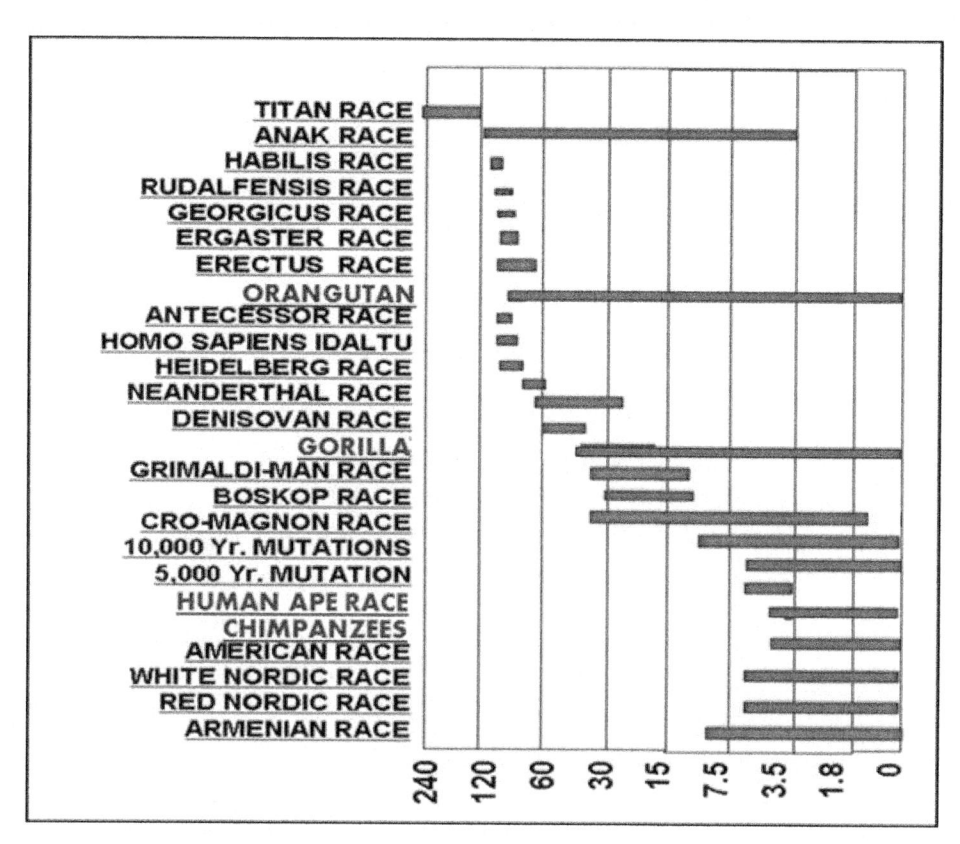

TITAN RACE	
ANAK RACE	
HABILIS RACE	
RUDALFENSIS RACE	
GEORGICUS RACE	
ERGASTER RACE	
ERECTUS RACE	
ORANGUTAN	
ANTECESSOR RACE	
HOMO SAPIENS IDALTU	
HEIDELBERG RACE	
NEANDERTHAL RACE	
DENISOVAN RACE	
GORILLA	
GRIMALDI-MAN RACE	
BOSKOP RACE	
CRO-MAGNON RACE	
10,000 Yr. MUTATIONS	
5,000 Yr. MUTATION	
HUMAN APE RACE	
CHIMPANZEES	
AMERICAN RACE	
WHITE NORDIC RACE	
RED NORDIC RACE	
ARMENIAN RACE	

240 120 60 30 15 7.5 3.5 1.8 0

The preceding chart shows the general timeframes of variations of humans and ape-men. Please notice chimpanzees and the group called human ape-men that appear around 5500 years ago. That will be a sad story, but it need to be told.

Homo Erectus

The Nephilimic human actions in genetic manipulation and their searching for limitations of genetics as the major goal seem to fit with the oddball characteristics of many of the really strange animals that were formed during the time of the dinosaurs and afterwards. This inventive group of scientists made some pretty amazing animals and some pretty stupid animals. While that is all fine and good, sometimes the Nephilim simply needed help. That help came in the form of the "6th Age man".

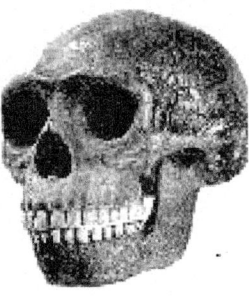

If the skull above looks like others you have seen, it is because they represent what we call the Homo Erectus. For some unexplainable, mysterious reason, there was a big jump in "evolution" between the animal called Homo-Habilis and this new being. The Habilis could walk on 2 feet, but he would not have been a good worker. Let's bring the Nephilimic people into the picture. The Nephilim had gone about as far as they could with apes in the Habilis structure and they needed help. They really could not change the major components of life. For instance, cross genus kind breeding could not cause procreation when animals were experimented on. The Habilis simply would not change to become more human. It didn't have an opposing thumb. It didn't have the powerful neck muscles, or the large occipital opening at the base of the skull. Its feet were still hand-like and his thighbones were curved like other apes. Then, all of a sudden-----humans changed. The changes were seemingly impossible, but somehow they happened. Scientists call the changed human HOMO-ERECTUS.

Brains and More Brains

Homo Erectus was the first true human of this line. His features were man-like including his teeth, pelvis, and legs. He was much larger than the 3.5-foot tall Habilis and his brain had swelled to over 800 cubic centimeters or almost twice that of his very recent predecessor. Those things didn't happen by chance and they all point to a very strong, very articulate, very manlike worker. The brain expansion was almost like the brain had gone into an evolution jet going thousands of years in the future while the same general shape and appearance looked **almost** like a reasonable progression. Don't confuse evolution with NEW CONSTRUCTION.

After God made this new being, the Nephilim immediately began griping again. I'm sure that the man that was created was a good worker, because his bone structure and articulation level tells us that. The Nephilim now wanted something different. They wanted to be worshipped like gods and this "God's new MAN being" was not worshipping the Nephilim like they expected and this odd man was not much of a free thinker. The Nephilim actually thought they wanted smarter humans. They felt they needed smarter humans for three reasons.

- According to the ancient texts, the first reason was so that they could do even more of the work.

- The second reason was so that the beings would worship them,
- And the third reason, sort of in the back of their minds, was so that they could become the expendable part of an army to eventually defeat God in another battle with heaven.

This new "human" was nothing like the Homo Habilis. For one thing his frontal lobe of his brain was fashioned similar to ours so that he most likely could speak and use language to transmit history, training, and civilization. Additionally his hips were made completely different than Habilis. Rather than having to strain at walking upright, his new bone structure was set up to almost always stand upright and even run on only 2 legs.

Characteristic found in Erectus	Habilis
Human Thumb	no
Brain size jumped by 50 percent almost overnight to 800cc	Only 400cc
Powerful human neck muscles	no
Human-like occipital opening	no
Human-like feet	no
Straight human-like thighbone	no
Smaller, more human brow-ridge	no
Rounded human-like mandible	no
Human-like canine teeth	no
Speaking	no
Transport of raw materials long distances	no
Very well made hammer and pick tools	no
Could run on 2 legs	no
Protruding human like nose	no
Vestigial ape-like cranial ridge	no

Neanderthal

Without adding in the Nephilimic overseers, nobody seems to be able to determine where the Neanderthal came from and no one can determine how it disappeared. Although it was very similar to the Homo Erectus, its brain again jumped in size and was now larger than even the brain of today's humans. Many other anomalous features make scientists wonder about this strange humanoid's appearance, but I think there is a logical answer. The Neanderthal was, evidently, the hybrid offspring of the union between 6th Age man and the Nephilim. I know that sounds like the easy "cop out" answer, but there are many bits of information to lead us to this conclusion. As shown in the table following there were marked changes that spontaneously occurred in this "new" human. The changes don't make sense. That is if you don't consider the introduction of Nephilim crossbreeding.

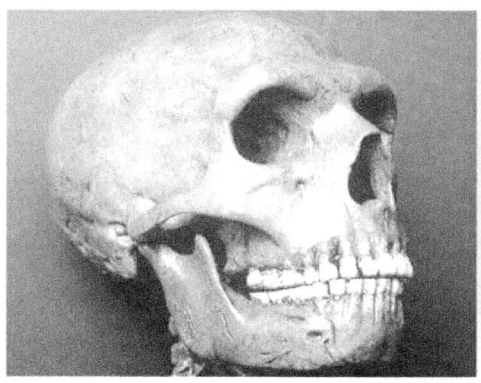

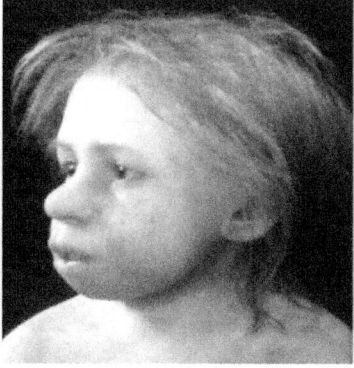

Characteristic found in Neanderthal	Erectus
Found with "Alien" genes that didn't come from Apes	no
Brain size jumped by 50 percent almost overnight to 1200cc	Only 800cc
Got an elongated Brain [for increased motor skills]	Round brain
Began to live in villages	no
Began to protect the sick	no
Began to bury the dead	no
Began to have religion	no
Had Big pronounced Nose	no
Loss of the vestigial cranial ridge	no

OK! The big nose doesn't show advancement, but I would imagine that the Neanderthal were proud of their protrusion and ostracized the Homo Erectus for having the apelike flat nose. The petite nose showed inferiority and they wore it with pride. The alien gene thing is really strange and needs to be explained. The explanation follows. None of the Neanderthal "alien genes" have been found in Erectus, but then again, to be fair, no DNA has been found. DNA of Neanderthal is another story.

Neanderthal's Alien Gene

The "homo-erectus" base was continuously manipulated genetically to characterize the perfect worker for the Nephilim and the Neanderthal was the ultimate achievement. Over the last 150 years, scientists have struggled to unravel the mystery of the Neanderthals without the acceptance of this important piece of the puzzle. Of course, their conclusions are very limited because they tried to separate science and religion. The first significant discovery was made in August 1856. A partial skeleton was found at the Feldhofer Cave in the Neander Valley, in Germany. This was the find that gave the species its name. Since then over 500 individuals have been found from over 80 sites in Europe, the Middle East and parts of Western Asia along with several hundred thousand stone tools. It wasn't until 1997 that a small scrap of DNA was discovered which showed "Alien Genetics" with respect to our own DNA or that of an ape. Neanderthal could not have come from either group "exclusively" as neither group contained portions of the DNA found in Neanderthal. This unexplainable feature greatly confused the already misaligned groups of Paleoanthopolgists. Besides the physical elements and no common ancestor, here are some of the things we have been told about the Neanderthal species as a social animal.

- Some of them were cannibalistic as determined from a Moula-Guercy, France site evidence.
- There was hybridization between Cro-Magnon and Neanderthal about 25 thousand years ago as evidenced from a recent Portuguese find showing many ambiguous characteristics.

Even though the Neanderthal, as a species, lived for many thousands of years, they continued to use rudimentary tools and weapons. This anomaly is very puzzling given the fact that Neanderthal had a larger brain than modern man, but there may be a good reason for this strange fact. A theory of this anomaly will be presented later.

The majority of the "pure Neanderthal" stayed in the European area. They began the custom of elongating their heads artificially, showing a strong reverence to some type of longheaded humans. Later we will also see the significance of this strange custom, so don't forget this element while we look at his brain.

Neanderthal Brain

While we are on the subject of Neanderthal heads, we need to discuss brains, because, like I said before, Neanderthal had a larger brain and the brain was shaped substantially different than the "Modern Man Brain". The Neanderthal brain was much longer as shown by the elongated skull on the right as compared to the modern skull on the extreme left.

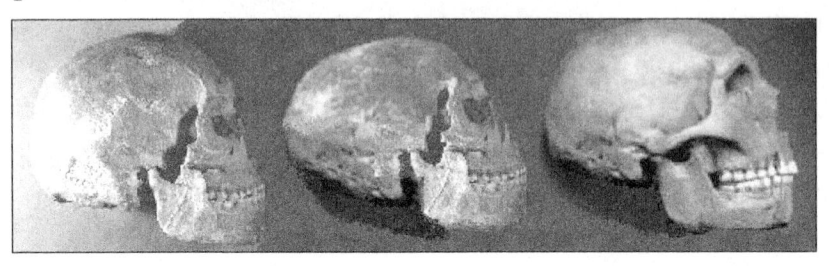

      Modern   European   Neanderthal

The chart below shows the general progression of brain size to humanoid type and mean period of existence. The vertical lines represent the range of brain sizes determined for each of the subgroups. Note the sharp slope as brain sizes began expanding faster and faster until the Neanderthal. By the way, this chart does not include the anomalous dolichocephalic giants that will not be introduced in this work. It only shows the "Normal species".

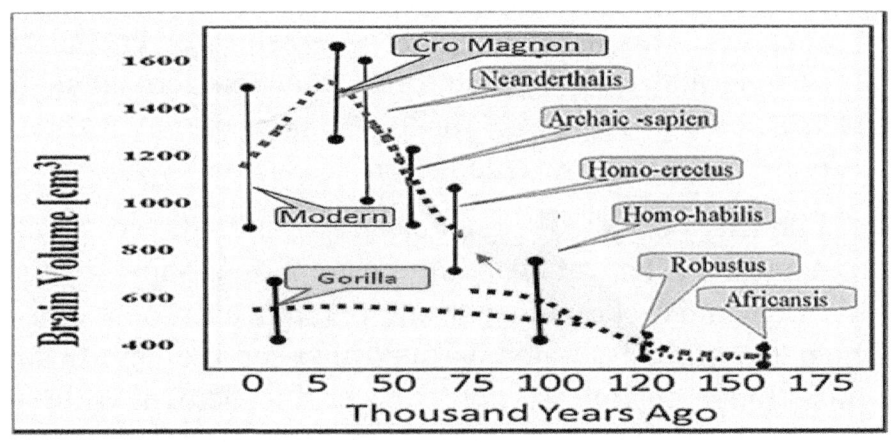

The picture below shows a modern skull with the typical 1400cc brain size and a Neanderthal Brain on the left with a brain size of 1500cc. This substantial brain size reduction

88

must be considered when investigating the development of humans.

European Neanderthal

To make things even more interesting, the brain shape of ancient European "homo sapien-sapiens", as shown by the middle skull image are more closely identified with the Neanderthal than those of the Middle Eastern homo-sapien-sapien [left] brains. This whole" long flat brain" and the "round brain" anomaly should be investigated further, because Neanderthal didn't make complex tools and his flat brain may tell us why.

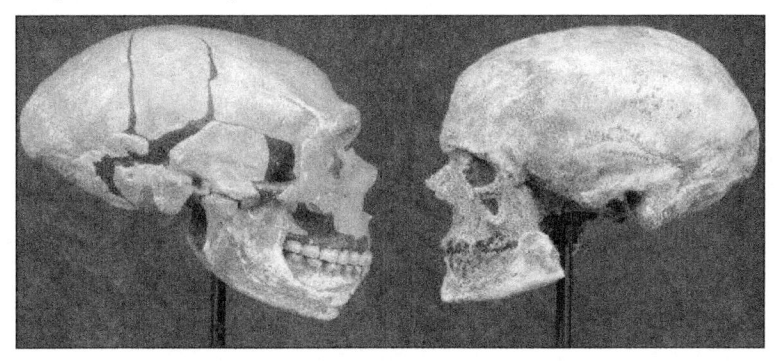

Neanderthal Brain Anomaly

The huge brain of this species means that Neanderthal was a smart individual. In some respects he was smarter than today's humans who suffer from brain atrophy. Our shrinking brain isn't important right now, but it will come up again, later.

Some will argue that having a large brain does not necessarily mean the individual is smart. That comment seems to be a crazy assertion, usually made by someone with a small brain.

It's like saying that the dinosaurs were smart because they had tiny brains. Even more than being smart, the difference in shape suggests something else. He had capabilities we do not have nor possibly ever had in our ancient past. I don't know what those were, but the large back portion of the Neanderthal brain suggests that they had to do with enhanced sight, hearing, and motor skills. That's right I said motor skills. He wasn't a lumbering individual and must have been able to perform maneuvers we cannot begin to achieve today with respect to hand-eye coordinated efforts. He had been engineered to be a fantastic worker for the Nephilim.

Neanderthal Articulation

According to a large amount of physical evidence, the Neanderthal could punch very clean holes through bones for talismans and they did this remarkable feat with very rudimentary tools. This by itself does not show enhanced articulation, but it is a clue. We may also notice that European craftsmanship is highly praised today and the European brains, at least the early ones, seem to be in between Neanderthal and the other "modern" human brains. Perhaps we should infer that a large back portion of the brain denotes enhanced articulation.

Neanderthal Creativity

The other thing that is noticeable is the fact that the "central creativity lobe" is smaller making the brain more flattened than that of Cro-Magnon and our current brains. This suggests that their creativity level was not up to our potential. Whenever the new creation was established, some of these features were not necessary and therefore were not integrated into the design of the man/hybrid. With less creativity came less advancement. Neanderthal made and used only very rudimentary tools even though he was very smart. The two don't seem to go together, but what we will find out is that this hybrid man may not have needed any special tools and his creativity level did not make him investigate newer ways to do things once an adequate method had been reached.

Lack of curiosity evidently killed this cat [I mean Neanderthal].

Neanderthal Worker

These very articulate, highly intelligent, extremely strong workers would have taken more time to develop his society with this lower level of creativity, but that did not mean that he wasn't very good at what he was made for. He was made to be a worker. He worked in huge mining fields that have been found around the world. He worked in the fields; he worked on construction sites; and he worked for the master race of Nephilim/Anak until the Adam/Cro-Magnon was created. Then, according to Biblical texts and other documents, within one generation, metalworking, war materials, use of colors, music, and other things were quickly discovered and used. As each new discovery was made by the Cro-Magnon/Adamic human. I can hear the Neanderthal saying---"Why didn't I think of that?" The reason was the shape of his brain.

Destined for Extinction

Besides his large, intelligent but uncreative brain, the Neanderthal was a true offshoot with no place to go, [or so it would seem]. The "evolutionary progression of apes and men are not nice *"modify every few years to make a BETTER animal"* thing, It is substantially more complex that those you may have seen in the past and then additions of the ancient humans, ancient giants, Nephilimic/Anak man, and Gigantopithecus add to the complexity and most of this is simply thrown away to support this uncontrolled evolution hypothesis. If a new creature comes along, it is thrown under the rug to make consensus scientist happy and generally destroy any hope of our children getting any meaningful information.

Gigantopithecus Ape-Man

Gigantopithecus is a well known offshoot and was actually was manufactured prior to the Neanderthal. In fact, he may have been modification of Homo Erectus with Anak gigantism genes inserted for scariness. Some even suggest it was this monster that was modified to "create" gorilla. He existed during the mid-Tertiary period; in what is now China, India, and Vietnam, These guys were the largest apes that ever lived, standing up to 10 feet and weighing up to 1,200 pounds. The first Gigantopithecus remains described by an anthropologist were found in 1935 by Ralph von Koenigswald in an apothecary shop. Fossilized teeth and bones are often ground into powder and used in some branches of Traditional Chinese medicine. This guy had huge teeth and bones so you could really make a lot of powder. Since then relatively few fossils have been recovered except for teeth. In 1955 forty-seven Gigantopithecus teeth were found among a shipment of 'dragon bones' in China. I don't know why they didn't think they were real dragon bones, but that is not part of this story. From there more teeth and a rather complete large mandible were found and by 1958, three mandibles and more than 1,300 teeth had been recovered.

Below is a size comparison and some of the stuff they have recovered on the following page. This would not be someone you would want to be made at you. Some claim this ape-ish hulk is none other than the big foot that has been seen over the last thousand years or so, but this guy was much bigger and dumber. We can assume if this was the branch that has been seen, we would have been able to catch a few.

Gigantopithecus (Temperate) **6' Tall Human**

The following collage shows the things that have been found so far. The tiny jawbone in the upper right corner of the collage is a human one.

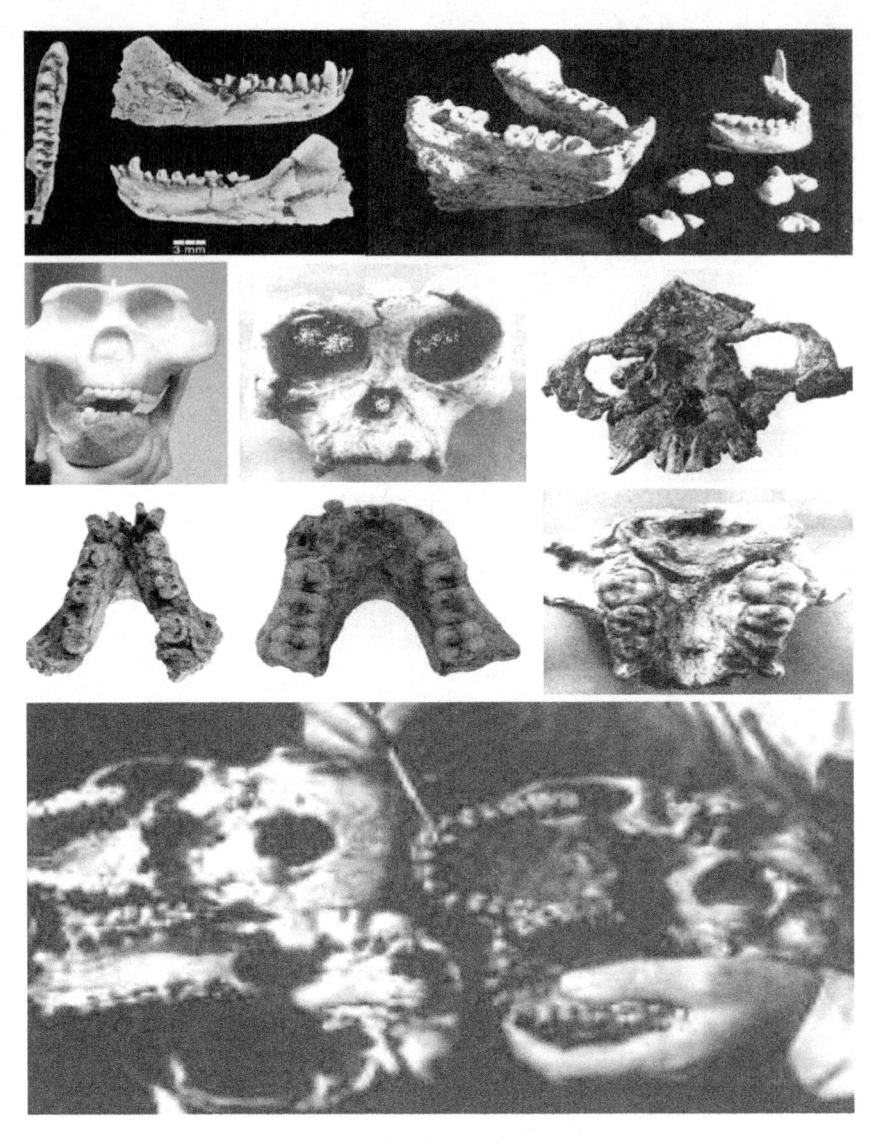

Big Foot

That sort of brings us to big foot and yeti. Around the world these stupid foot prints keep showing up along with the occasional sighting of what looks to be a gigantic ape like biped. Most people simply laugh and we can imagine a guy with a fake footprint making device laughing at researchers, but we will see later that people that looks similar to Sasquatch lived about 5000 years ago and was integrated into society.. They didn't called them sasquatch. They were the Vanara people. We will get to them later.

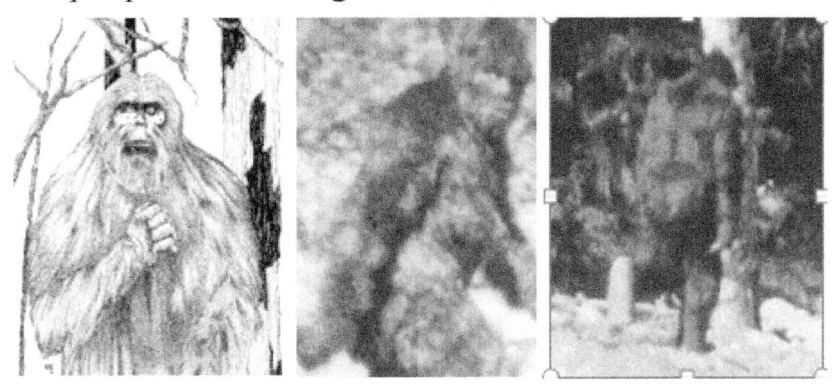

All over the United States, Canada, and many other parts of the world the same apelike things has been spotted and tracked even the skullcap of one from the Himalayas is now being protected by Buddhist monks. It would be difficult to say these guys don' exist especially with the Gigantopithecus all over the place. It simply means that the geneticists of very ancient times survived the flood to reestablish the breed after the Pleistocene Extinction 10 thousand years ago. On the following page are just a few of the dozens and dozens of these massive footprints that are becoming more prevalent every year. Wait a minute! The yeti and big foot aren't 10 foot tall; they must be an offshoot of the Meganthropus.

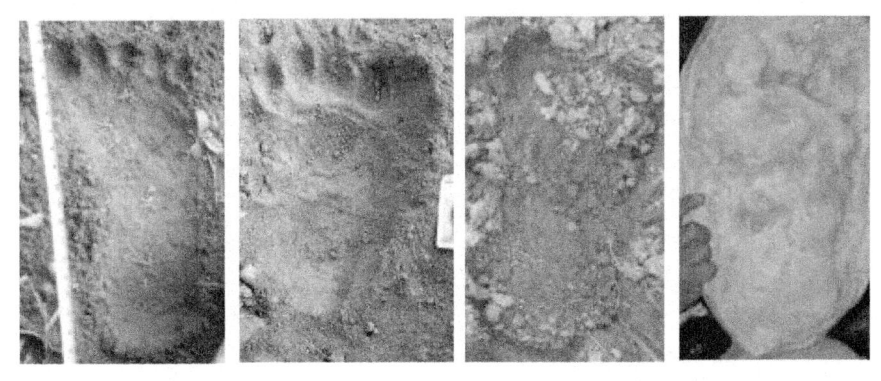

Every year more and more of these thing show up[and more and more video as something appears to run away from intruders. Where the images were take, footprints are left.

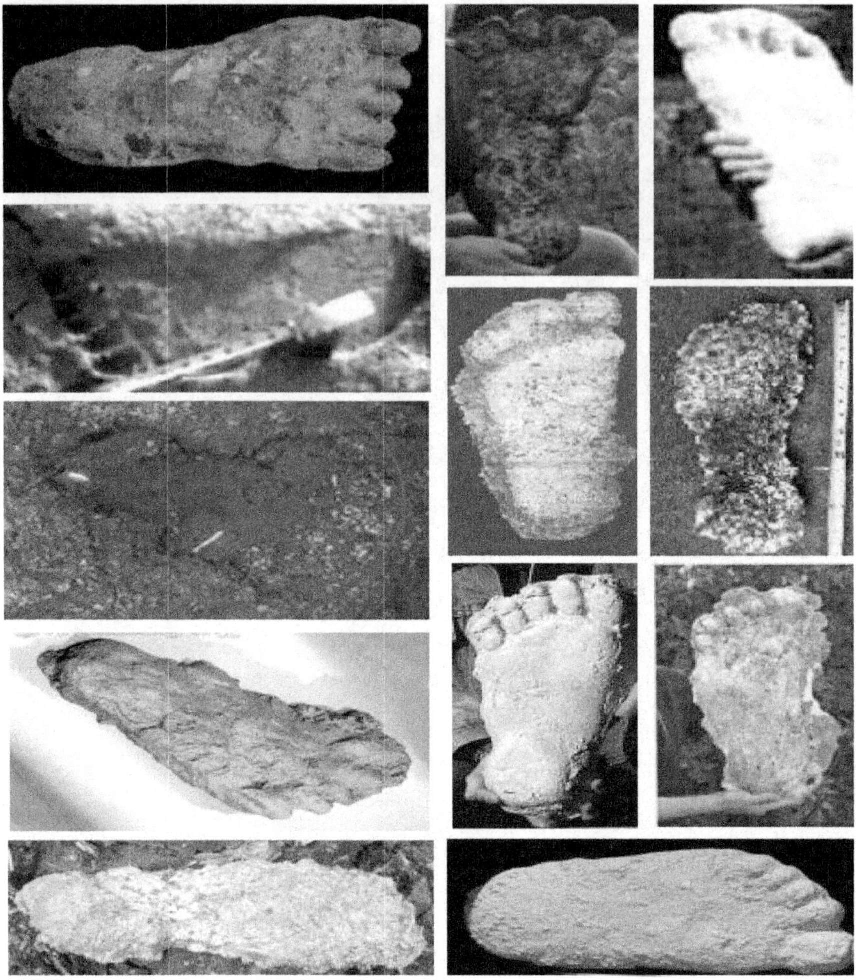

Meganthropus Ape-man

After the Gigantopithecus the geneticists decided to make something slightly smaller and the Meganthropus ape-man was created. This guy lived in the same general area as the previous model but he was more human looking and only 8 feet tall. As the skull shows, his teeth were much more human like, but the ridge along the brain was similar to that of today's apes. Certainly not as drastic as the gorilla, but this guy looks ape-ish for sure.

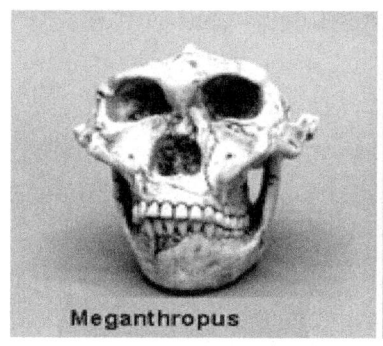

Meganthropus

The first large jaw fragment was first found in 1941 by von Koenigswald. Unfortunately, Koenigswald was captured by the Japanese in World War II, but fortunately he managed to send a cast of the jaw to a scientist named Franz Weidenreich. Weidenreich described and named the specimen in 1945. It was the largest hominid jaw then known. The jaw was roughly the same height as a gorilla's, but was much thicker. The size was 2/3 the size of Gigantopithecus, which was still twice as large as a gorilla Meganthropus had a cranial capacity of around 900cc and roamed the earth during the mid-Tertiary period so he was here while Gigantopithecus and Homo Habilis were making their mark. A couple of the skulls found were somewhat odd in that they had a double temporal ridge. That's the ape ridge on the skull of the large apes. I have no idea what that means, but it is interesting just the same. If you are like me you might be thinking that this Meganthropus character didn't die off 90 thousand years ago and he's still out there, somewhere putting his big feet on forest pathways.

Chimpanzee

We will talk about these guys later, but right now let's describe them. Chimpanzees don't have much of a past according to evolutionist as their characteristics are different than other apes in a substantial way and unlike the characteristics of the gorilla, baboon, spider monkey, lemur, tarsier, orangutan, gibbon, and tamarind. Let me show you the recognized "everything-was-created-at-one-time" chart that is now gaining acceptance again. This variant was done in 1994, but is generally the same as I showed earlier. [See the following page]. Anyway, the thing that stands out most about chimpanzees is tool making and use. Our closest living relative, the chimpanzee, uses tools spontaneously, both in the wild and in nature. Wooden tools are usually used and if a stone is used, they do not shape it for use. They also train their children to use tools. Mother chimpanzees give their child a good hammer. She would leave nuts near the anvil [cupped area in a rock] or put the nut on the anvil and leave the tool nearby, to provide incentive for the young animal to try to crack the nut. If the child hits wrong, the mother quickly picks up the nut, cleans the anvil, and replaces the nut correctly to be smashed, but she still makes the child to the work and learn the actions. To get bugs out of a tree, a chimpanzee simply takes a blade of grass and sticks it in a "bug hole" in a tree as far as they can get it and then it waits. Soon, when he brings it out a succulent larva or bug is on the blade eating away until the Chimp chomps. In captivity, chimpanzees also use tools. When researchers hung food in their enclosure, they acted sort of like anthropoid engineers, stacking up crates and using a pole to reach suspended food. In a silly situation, one chimpanzee in the wild became the dominant male through his use of empty kerosene cans that he banged together to intimidate larger males. If you are smaller, you need to carry a big kerosene can I suppose. Other complex actions of these marvelously engineered animals include meat eating, tool making, deliberate planning, warfare, cannibalism, formation of coalitions, adoption of non-related chimps, exploitation of social situations, the use of medicinal plants, and technology transfer. These don't seem to make sense.

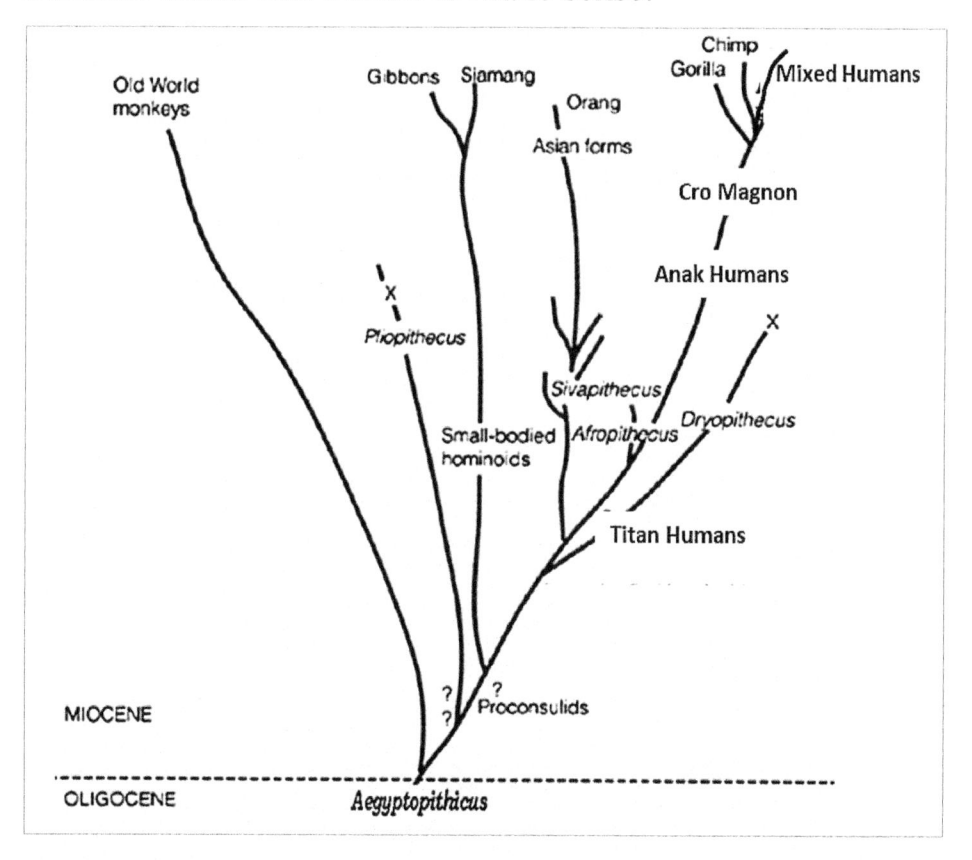

All this stuff is fine and good, but if there isn't more proof of ancient humans scientists walking around I will have to continue. Without scientists, we might have to go back to the evolution theory and simply deal with it. Luckily there are tons and tons of pieces of evidence and I'm not going to fill up this book with all of it, but I am going to present a small amount just to let you know that civilized humans roamed the entire earth even during the time of the dinosaurs. These people included scientists that not only were capable of designing animals, but also developed techniques for nuclear war, carpentry and brick working, complex manufacturing, and all types of things. They wore normal clothing including shoes and they WALKED WITH DINOSAURS.

Evidence Of Ancient Engineers

Very ancient humans left their mark on the world as early as the Jurassic Period. The creatures in the ancient communities looked like us, walked like us, made things like us, but were here before the time that they could have been here---or so many SCIENTISTS say. From at least the Jurassic Period substantial amounts of evidence show that humans walked with dinosaurs, killed dinosaurs, shot each other and animals with projectiles like bullets, built huge underground mines, designed and crafted intricate objects like bells and toys, and wore shoes similar to those used today.

Manufactured goods- Investigators have found toys, jewelry, and construction tools from the Mesozoic Era. Some of the objects found include the bell, a workman's ladle, and even a hammer with a coalified handle as shown below. Additional Mesozoic finds include a battery encased in a geode. A gold chain in a lump of coal a thimble, and even a small clay doll attest to their civilization.

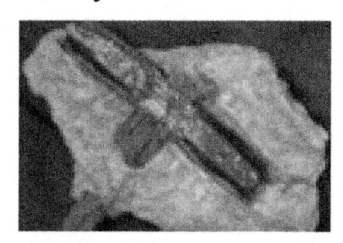

Heavy Wheeled Transport-In Turkey was found dozens of tracks on Lava rock estimated to be from extremely ancient times. The wheeled transports were so heavy, massive ruts in the rock are still extant. The tracks cut across the landscape of the Phrygia Valley as shown below.

Malta Ruts-Very similar interesting and <u>mysterious tracks exist in other locations</u> of the world, notably in the Maltese archipelago. These ancient grooves continue to puzzle researchers. Some of the strange tracks of Misrah Ghar il-Kbir deliberately plunge off cliffs or continue off land and into the ocean so they were made when the Island was part of the mainland. It is not yet known who made the tracks shown below.

One might ask, "Who made these enigmatic tracks, and why?"

Utah Shoeprint-1968-The picture is of a fossilized, 10-½ inch long human sandal print found next to a small human's footprints. Live trilobites were crushed by the sandal in the same stone before fossilization. Columbia Union College made studies on the fossil an attested to its authenticity. The Age was Mesozoic. The circles show the location of two unfortunate trilobite carcasses. Unfortunately, trilobites became extinct during the Mesozoic Era. Two lost their lives when this shoed person carelessly walked over and killed them. The image to the left is a blow up of the front one.

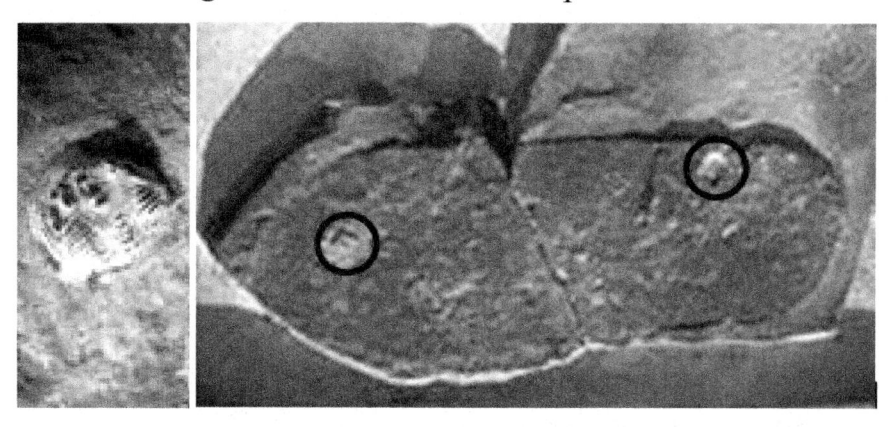

Nevada 1927-A Jurassic period sandal sole print was found in a coal seam. The only way for the print to be there is for the person to have walked on the area before the coal was coal. Even the impressions of the threading holding the shoe together could be discerned. [See left image]

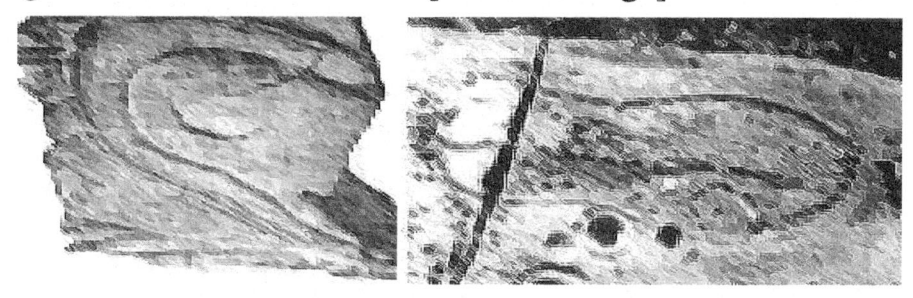

Washington State-This photo [above right] was taken in northern Washington State and was reportedly found with another partial imprint. It is the 16-inch long shoe print of a large individual. The rock itself was determined to be early Tertiary Period, so the person wearing the shoe must have been there a long time ago.

Tanzania-All of the findings of human ancestors in Africa are tainted by the desire to show evolution. Note the forward direction of the human footsteps next to the smaller back and forth footprint pattern of an apelike ancestor. The tracks are dated to mid Tertiary period and show Normal humans lived in the area.

Australia-Since the first finding of human fossil impressions there have been over 90 hand and footprint impressions found. It has been estimated that the ancient Australian humans were over 14 feet tall by the size of the impressions. The footprints included those that were obviously children and full size adults with footprints as large as 24 inches long by 12 inches wide across the toes. The handprints are similar with the largest about 16 inches between out stretched fingers. While some of the imprints have been dated to late Tertiary period, others are substantially older showing the consistent inconsistency of the "survival of the fittest evolution model"

Kentucky 1938-Three pairs of tracks [human] were sunk in gray sandstone [once a sandy beach during the Cretaceous Period]. Photomicrograph studies showed that the tracks were not manufactured artificially or recently and again we fear we have been lied to. [See below left]

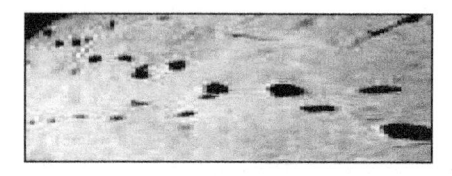

Texas-Texas is full of sites —In total there were over 200 dinosaur prints and about 60 human prints found in the same area. The largest human print was over 16 inches long. The group of prints shown is at Glen Ross Texas and it has 14 human and 134 dinosaur tracks together. It has been estimated to have been made during the Cretaceous period. [See previous right]

Other sites show similar ancient, completely upright walking humans. The following collage show some of the more famous petrified beach walks proving ancient humans went to the beach and that dinosaurs like the same beaches as humans.

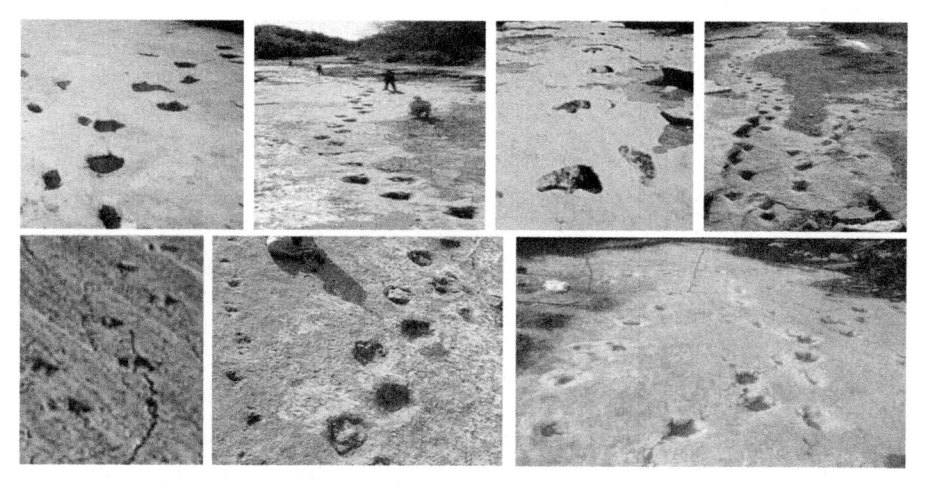

Australian Humans and Dinosaurs-According to "Ancient Secrets of the Bible" human *footprints commingled with Cretaceous dinosaur* prints were found in Australia. [See below]

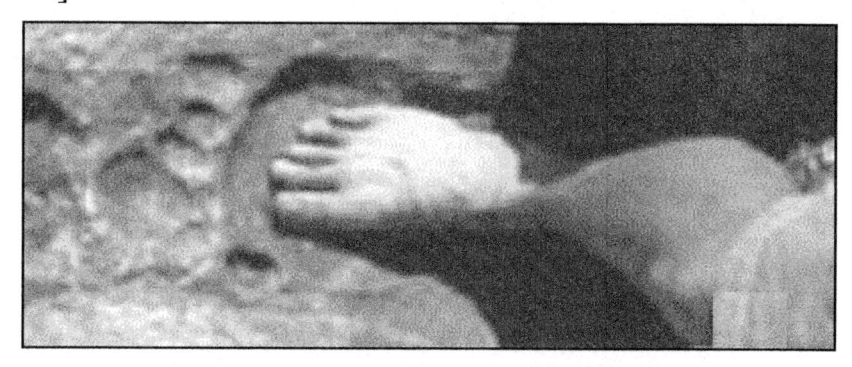

They have actually found hundreds of these prints. One is shown to the right the people were somewhat larger than us, but they lived with the dinosaurs for sure.

Russia-1983-According to the "Moscow News", human footprints were found alongside and in the same strata as three toed dinosaur tracks. The estimated age is Cretaceous.

Colorado 1867-Homo-Sapien style human remains were found imbedded in a silver vein at a depth of 400 feet Estimated age that the vein was formed was during the Jurassic Period.

California 1866-A Homo-Sapien type human skull was found. From fossils and **shells wedged between portions of the skull** it was dated to be later Tertiary Period.

Italy 1958-A Modern human jawbone was found in a coal shaft at a depth of 600 feet- The estimated age of the coal was early Tertiary Period. Try to pack 600 feet of coal in a few thousand years---It is simply impossible.

California 1877-A metal Mortar and Pestle was found **under some lava beds** 300 feet deep. The mortar is about 4 inches in diameter. The estimated age of the objects was determined to be Early Tertiary Period. [See next left]

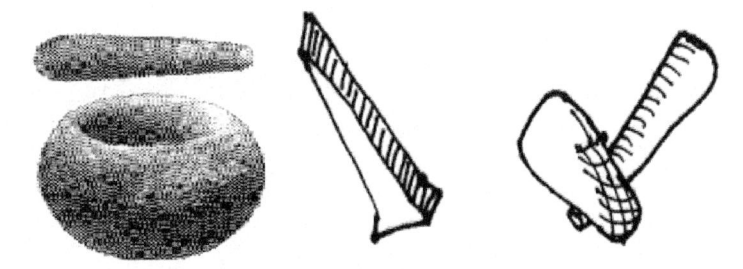

California 1851-A cut iron nail shown above, was found inside a **quartz crystal**. Estimated age of the crystal was mid Tertiary period. Reported in the "Illinois Springfield

Republican", it was very similar to those we use today as the sketch illustrates.

Texas 1976-Another ancient Hammer was found [shown preceding right] alongside dinosaur prints. The composition of the hammer was 97% iron. The estimated age of the adjacent footprints was dated to be Cretaceous. [Just when did the Iron Age start anyway?]

Nevada 1869-The remains of a 2-inch long metal screw were found inside a block of **feldspar**. The calculated age of the stone was early Tertiary Period. The screw itself was completely decomposed, but the rock contained a perfect mold of what had been inside.

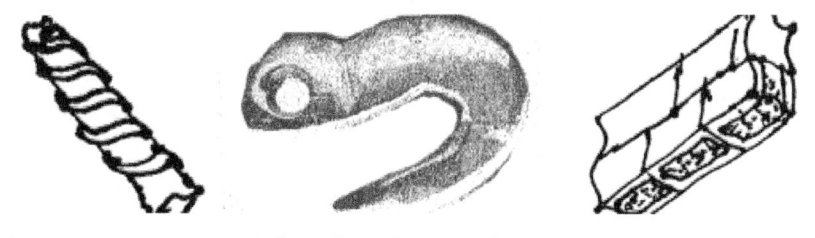

Illinois 1851-At a depth of 120 feet a copper device like a boat hook came up during a well drilling. A "similar" one is shown.

Oklahoma-1928-A block wall was found almost 2 miles deep in a coal mine. Each block was 12 x 12 x 12 inches polished on the outside and filled with gravel on the inside-There were multiple reports over 150 yard length of the same wall. The estimated age of the wall was Cretaceous. [See the diagram on the right above.]

Philadelphia 1829-A 30 cubic foot piece of marble was excavated from a depth of 60 feet. Inside the marble was a straight edged rectangular indentation. After a section of the marble was carefully removed it was found that 2 distinct heavily engraved letters similar to an "I" and a "U" eleven inches long and 5.8 inches deep were on a square base. The estimated age was Cretaceous.

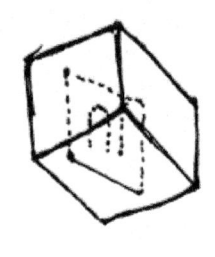

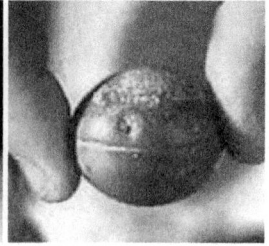

Britain-1844-The head of a metal nail was found encased in a 9-inch thick block; similar to the illustration, much of the nail was gone. [2nd preceding image]

Germany 1886-An Iron Cube was found 2.6 x 2.6 x 1.9 inches. 4 sides were flat and the other 2 were convexed with groves incised around the flat sides. The estimated age of the object was late Cretaceous. [3rd preceding]

South Africa 1970s-Over 200 "1 to 4" inch **iron spheres** were found. Some were cored with a spongy material inside. Some were formed with fine grooves etched into the circumference. The spheres were found in beds of Pyrophyllite with an estimated age of before the Cretaceous period. [4th preceding]

Coin in Coal

A coin-like object embedded in a lump of carboniferous coal was found and was reported in "Strand Magazine" in 1901. The coal would have been laid during the Cretaceous Period. [No; there wasn't a date on the coin. See below left]

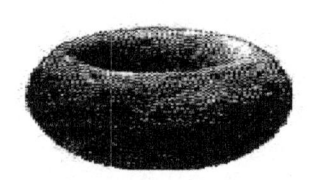

California 1866-Another stone mortar was found. From fossils and shells wedged between portions of a skull also found with it has been dated to be mid Tertiary Period. [Preceding middle]

Iowa-1897-A large stone [2x2x1feet] with multiple faces of an old man carved on it and a grid pattern on the remaining area was found 130 feet down in a coalmine. The estimated age was Cretaceous. [Preceding Right]

Ohio 1869-A slate wall was uncovered in a coal mine shaft at a depth of 100 feet. The wall was covered in strange letters. The letters were raised and well defined and the coal around the letters contained the impressions. Each letter was 3/4 inches long and arranged in lines of about 25 letters. The estimated age was Jurassic.

1880 Colorado-According to the "American Antiquarian", inside a lump of coal, 300 feet deep, was found a perfectly formed thimble.

Morrisonville, USA-1891-A 10-inch long, 8 carat gold **chain** was found encased in coal estimated to be Jurassic.

Armargosa Desert 1961-On the edge of the Desert was found a geode. Inside was found an iridescent stone with a 2mm x 17mm long **metal rod**. [You know Geodes must be old. See next left]

Pennsylvania 1937-A woman named Myrna Burdick found a spoon among ash from burnt coal. The ashes had not been disturbed after a large piece of coal was burned, but when they fell apart, the spoon was noticed among them

Pennsylvania-At the same site as was found the Jurassic Human bones embedded in coal, there was found a handle for some type of tool. The handle was coalified just like the sample from Texas. [See following middle]

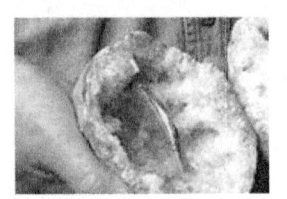

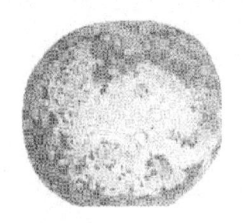

France, 1862 Man-made chalk balls were found near Leon and were estimated to be very early Tertiary Period. The balls were almost perfectly round and could not have been naturally produced. [See above right]

1791 Germany-According to "The Fossils of South Down", inside a piece of flint was found an "Ancient Brass Pin".

France 1786-1788-Coins, tools and pieces of columns were brought up from areas below 11 different beds of limestone, which were estimated to be very early Tertiary Period.

Aluminum finds- An intricatre piece of an aluminum gear was fouind in Russia and a really stranger aluminum thing with perpendicularly drill holes was found near Transylvasnia. Aluminum was reintroduced to th eworld in 1840s so these anceint peole knew a thing or two. One thing we can be pretty sure of is that they kneqw about electricity.

Batteries, Growing Blocks and Nuclear Plants

I know all of the preceding things might just be coincidences. Maybe a thousand animals happened to peck a stone and finally something was made or who knows, but we found more. The picture to the right below is some type of power conversion device found **inside** a geode, in California. Below the geode is a drawing of x-rays of the geode showing the elemental parts. These include a spring, core, plate, and electrical insulator. The same parts as you would expect in a battery. Maybe this is a new way to package batteries, but it takes a long time to complete the package.

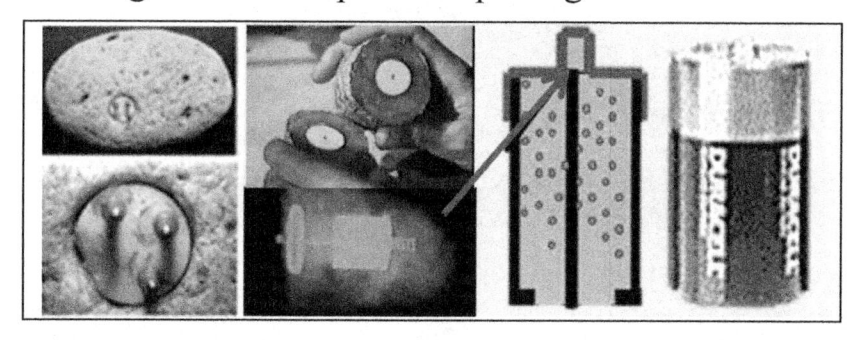

Both of the objects are extremely ancient and certainly before we originally thought that everyone used electricity. The central metal core surrounded by the white material looks like a battery, although some even attribute the structure to that of a spark plug. Whatever it was, it was electrical. On the left is a drawing of the parts and a size comparison to a standard D-cell battery.

Growing Buildings-The picture to the right [following] has been determined to be a floor section that is thousands of years old. The reason this is of interest is that it shows a remarkable capability to "Grow Stones". These stones were grown at such an ancient time, the central core is almost completely gone, but the outside lattice structure of this ancient floor can still be seen in the West Virginian countryside. These would have been floors and walls used by the ancient Titan or Anak rulers. The joints between each waffle pattern can be easily seen today. Each of the blocks is layered as though the blocks had been grown in place rather than being quarried at a distant sight. In the close-up shown, note how close together each of the blocks is positioned to adjacent ones. Not even a needle could pass between their interfaces. The interior of each of the floor stones was of a softer material and eventually was eaten away.

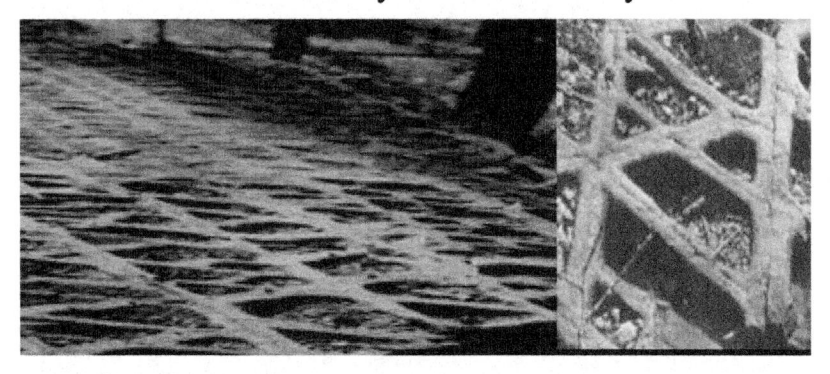

More West Virginia-The image below left, shows a West Virginian artifact that is very curious indeed. Note that the centers of the blocks are worn away and there is little or no space between the various "Rock rims" that are still visible. It is as if the rocks were covered in a hard substance that grew to meet adjacent rocks.

Oklahoma Grown Building-We find the same thing in Oklahoma. The "Grown blocks" in this Oklahoma Wall shown to the right, are believed to have been part of an ancient plant of some kind, but most of it has now weathered away. If the blocks were not grown in place, where did the people find these perfectly matching stones that have not been externally shaped? We can tell the stones were not worked because the outer layer of ringed material on each block has not been violated. It is believed that some of these sites might have been processing plants for raw materials including Copper and possibly Uranium from the New Mexican fields. Additional sites show these same types of "grown blocks" [see below]. Additional sites around the world including Peru and Australia assure us this was a common construction methodology of these ancient people.

Similar civilization in Brazil, Peru, Mexico, India, Egypt, and other sites show highly civilized people around the world. Below left is a PreInca wall showing higher density rock along the outside of the stone and a very similar rock from Australia showing the layers from buildup.

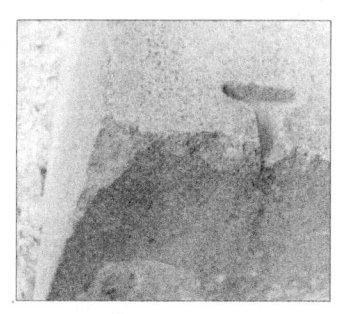

Many other items have been found and more shoeprints many, many footprints from the Cretaceous period, clothing marks, taxidermy of dinosaur evidence, handprints, and on and on we could go, but this book is about the apes so I'm going to concentrate on the whole hominid lineage. These geneticists probably were just like we are today. They moved some guanine in a DNA strand and voila!!! Something strange happened. Sometimes it was good and sometimes – not so good. If you remember in the 1980s, some genetic specialist designed an animal that ate oil. It was going to be the savior of animal life being choked to death by oil spills. To this date, the bacteria thing has never been loosed into the environment, because we have no idea what it could do to the world. I think that some of the animals that were created in the olden days were let loose when they should not have been. I believe that one of the "creations" of these guys that was accomplished a mere 7 thousand years ago almost destroyed the earth at that time and it even made more ape-like beings. That story is coming up later. Right now we are back in the time before and after the Heaven War and men needed fancy weapons. Therefore a huge nuclear war machine emerged. We find evidence that in all the major wars [the one before the Cretaceous Extinction, the one before the Pleistocene Extinction and the Bharata War all were fueled by this horrible killing capability. I know we are looking for something that is over 100 thousand years old, but many processing plants have been found. Do to the unusual requirements for this type of thing they were all placed in Oklo, Gabon, Africa.

Ancient Nuclear Plants or the Ancients

This is the last thing I want to bring up about this ancient time Researchers accidentally found 16 uranium processing plants all along the same nearby deposits of uranium and they all show signs of use as enriched uranium would have made some nasty weapons. While impossible to date nuclear stuff with nuclear decay dating, by location it has been estimated that the plants were designed BEFORE the Cretaceous Era. The design of the plants is so remarkable, there is **no nuclear fallout**. I know you were thinking these people were so backward, they had to rely on simple batteries for power, but I'm talking about nuclear plants, bombs, nasty wars etc. While built during this time, these plants were, evidently used over the years by others. Very quickly, scientists backpedaled and came up with the story that these were all *naturally occurring nuclear plants*, just like any other natural nuclear plants. Wait a minute!!! There aren't any! By comparing the percentage of Uranium 238, the reactors were estimated to have produced on the order 0f 1,000 megawatts, comparable to modern plants. All this could have been used to light houses or for war. The normal Uranium 238 was "processed" to Plutonium and "enriched" to Uranium 235 allowing energy to be provided and used [by someone]. The following graphic shows where the processing took place. I know it just looks like blobs, but believe, me this was put to use in the olden days and we have proof to look at later as it would not just be used by the Titans, but also the group called the Anak and finally it was used in the most devastating war of the modern Age.

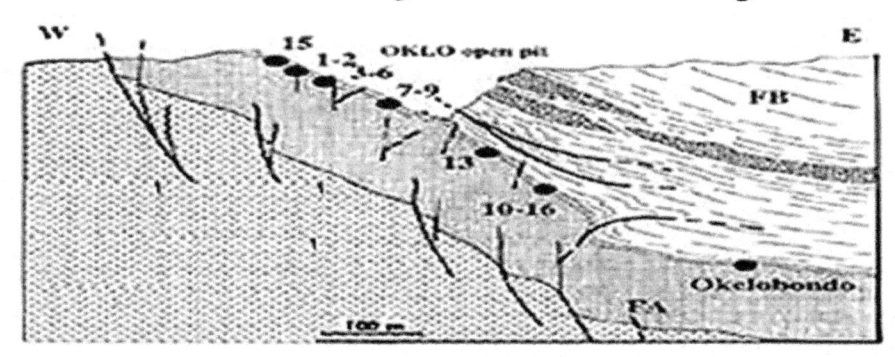

This brings us to genetics of these ancient people. Huge animals were made, smaller animals had to be made after the War because the earth rotation slowed, but more and more and more animals were pushed out. For some reason, our nutty evolutionists keep trying to push evolution rather than manufacture, but evolution cannot be made to make sense. Before we take a quick look at evolution, let me just stress something else here that we will investigate further later. Anytime nuclear byproducts are released into the air, mutations occur. One might think that one of the mutations could be called Chimpanzee. Forget I said anything and chimpanzees are coming for awhile as we are still in the Tertiary Period strangely, we find people and animals being shot with what appears to be bullets or killed with axes.

In Russia and extinct Auroch was found with a similar high speed projectile hole in its forehead which is believed to have been put there during the Pleistocene [See the following collage]. A similar hole was found in the same type animal in Zambia and other signs of hostilities. Most had a tiny hole going in and much larger exit destruction. Please notice something that might be bad. Many of the bullet holes are from point blank range given the entrance hole positions as if done by a contract killer. I wonder if it was some form of ancient mafia.

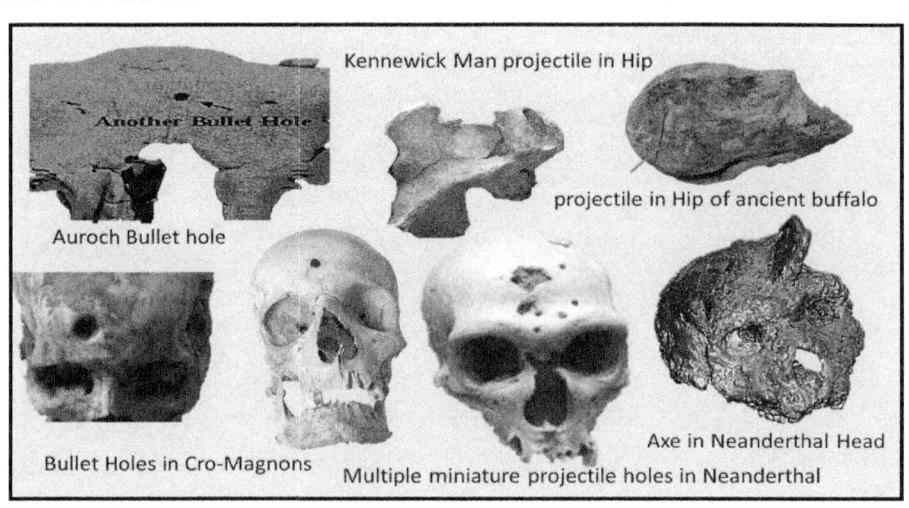

Some scientists started looking for holes and found bullet holes in skulls of Cro-Magnon and earlier people, pointing to the use of high speed projectile weapons used by the Anak people. Here are just a few more examples.

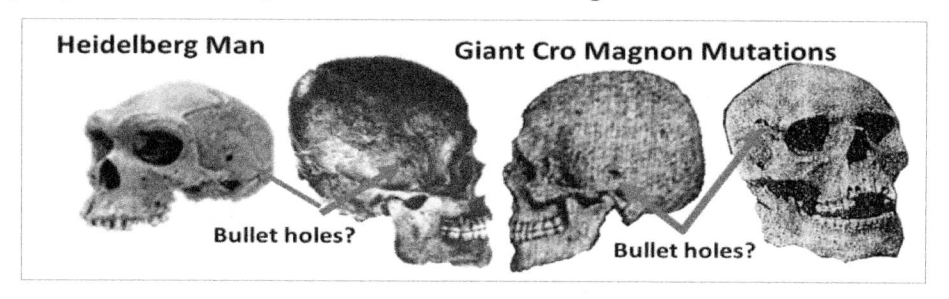

Heidelberg Man — Bullet holes?
Giant Cro Magnon Mutations — Bullet holes?

Still more apparent bullet holes in a Cro Magnon, Neanderthal, and a Paracas Anakim show it was a bad time.

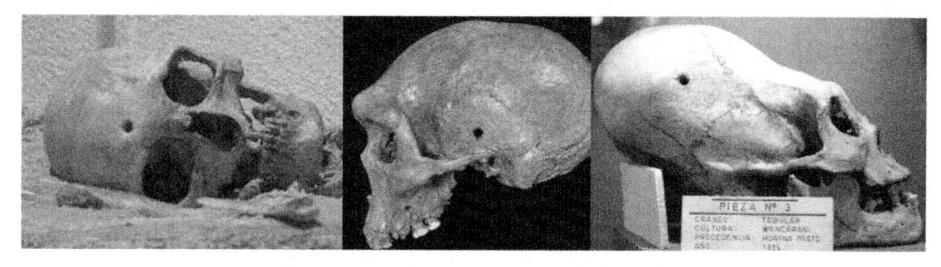

I provided these things to let you understand that the Homo-Gigantus and the larger Anak were highly civilized and were great scientists and engineers. Think about a society with modern capabilities and extremely long lifetimes. That combination when added to biology spells trouble. Instead of looking at the obvious, many scientists still cling to the crazy science of survival of the mistakes or evolutionary mistakes.

Scientists Push Evolution

I know that many of you believe in evolution simply because some smart scientist that had been studying evolution his whole life told you how it all went together. Don't be blinded by the things that fit, look for the things that don't.

Pterodactyls Don't Fit-Have you ever wondered why the Pterodactyl was supposedly created or evolved such that it could not fly and the only way it could hunt was to fly?????? When people tell you these things, don't just agree because they are scientists, ask questions. The answer must have been that this mighty creature could fly even though its structure is too heavy for it to have even accomplished it.

Stupid Bird Heads Don't Fit-If evolution and survival of the fittest were the only controlling factors for survival and existence, why are there so many surviving animal types and why are there so many traits that are generally so useless. By the way, why would animals be so vastly varied and strange unless a group was experimenting with different things? Let's look at birds over the years. All those topknots and things were not helpful to those birds. They were mistakes and the creator God would not have made mistakes. Take, for instance, the Toucan. What in the world is that beak useful for? It makes it more difficult for it to survive, but there is it a big chunk of useless beak.

In the following collage are some of the reconstructions of bird ancestors. Can you tell which came first? Most of the unusual characteristics are completely useless, but somehow the "bird" survived during the preflood days. I like the one in the bottom leftr that big bone topknot makes it look like the woody-woodpecker cartoon character and I guess it could have been used as a rudder, but if he turned his head to look at something while flying it could be very dangerous. Seriously, these heads show major mistakes in genetics that survived just like the Toucan as "survival of the LEAST fit" shows mistake after mistake.

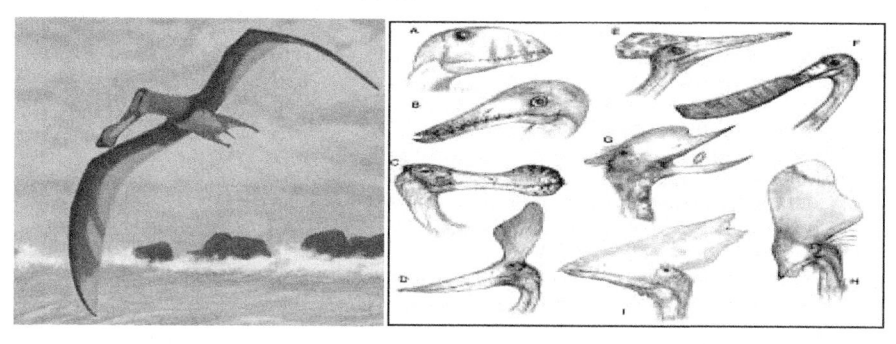

Stupid Partial Birds Don't Fit-Birds weren't the only mistakes of the ancient world. The misfit cross-animals that were neither bird nor true lizard looked like they were designed just for fun. Lizards with bird beaks abounded and lizards with feathers must have been plentiful, however, most of these have only been found in China. The geneticists in that country must have had fun during the early years.

The Ovirator looked like a parrot from the neck up, but a lizard for the most part in the body. [See next left] This is no missing link. It is a simple DNA mistake. These mistakes would not have survived unless some controlling caretaker assumed responsibility of establishing breeding colonies of these exotic pets.

Here are a couple more manipulated animals.

The Avimimus bird head lizard had rudimentary wings to go along with his beak. Of course the "wings" were totally useless. [See above middle]

Caudipteryx, not only had the bird beak and wishbone, this 3 foot tall bird-lizard had a gizzard according to the stomach contents found. [See above right]

Some may try to suggest that these are examples of crossover animals, but they make no sense as survival of the fittest would not let these useless animals survive. What does support the weirdness is random, sometimes thoughtless genetic experimentation. Sometimes they tried to design the biggest creature; sometimes the ugliest; sometimes the most unusual.

Many of these creatures show thoughtless genetic experimentation.

Let's go from weird to weirder.

Microrator-Gui

One mistake was the 4 winged bird-lizards as shown next. Just imagine trying to flap 4 legs at the same time. The Anak scientists were probably embarrassed to even show this mistake.

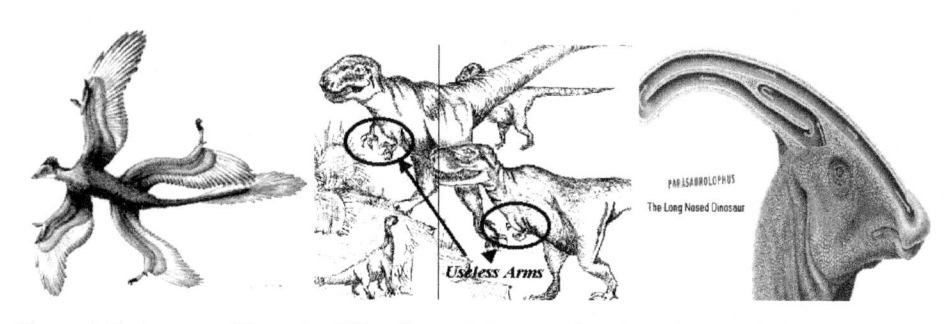

Stupid Arms Don't Fit-Speaking of mistakes with arms, we have got to look to the time before the Heaven War at the Tyrannosaurus Rex. Previously, it was determined to be the highest form of predator, but now we know differently. His arms are too short. Although he could run, if he fell it was an almost impossible situation for him to get back up. It was possible, but the energy expended would have been tremendous and many would not have survived. The new picture of the Rex is that of a clean-up animal like a vulture. The stupid thing was Big, strong, fast, and it mistakenly had tiny little arms. I saw a documentary indicating that the tiny arms reduced the weight on the legs so they were necessary. Anyone looking at the huge, heavy, hulking head and saying the arms got shorter to allow the creature to stand is somehow not seeing the big picture. T-Rex was another thoughtless genetic manipulation experiment. This time the geneticists were in North America. [See preceding middle]

Long Noses Don't Fit-Sometimes "evolved features" are recognizable as mistakes. A Dinosaur mistake to be considered would be the long nosed Dinosaur. His nose is over four times as long as his head and was curled back on itself. It was completely useless and there is no evidence to suggest that other dino-features evolved from this mistake. [See preceding right] The nose couldn't be used as a battering ram like the horn extensions of other animals. It was just a long nose. For those who would suggest that this is the father of the elephant with his useful nose/hand, it would be improbable that the thing would have evolved from this characteristic to the dangly one of today. Let me repeat this factor. This type of mistake probably didn't come from an omnipotent creator, nor did it come from an evolutionary process. This was a genetic mistake that happened to procreate for a time. "Ancient Humans" practiced Genetic manipulation over and over again. Although that seems to be a rash statement, it only makes sense. Beside the "no mistakes by God argument, a couple of the other reasons are given below:

Stupid Legs Don't Fit-The dinosaurs and birds were weird alright, but what about other animals of today? Let's take grasshoppers and butterflies, for instance. Their legs are being used for just about everything and it doesn't seem right.

Leg Tasting-Who would create an animal **with "taste buds" on its legs**? Now it seems dumb, but when the butterfly was created, experimentation was done on every level. It reminds me of the haphazard DNA experimentation we [20th century scientists] have done that caused wings to grow in place of eyes in a fruit-fly.

Leg Hearing-Then the "creators", or should I say experimenters, got to the grasshopper and decided to put grasshopper **ears on the legs**. Not only does that seem like a crazy place to put them, just think how loud it sounds to the grasshopper when he makes his leg scraping sound. I know you can probably come up with hundreds of oddities that make no sense with respect to any type of evolution process, but these are funny and appear to be jokes played on the unsuspecting animal. If you really want to see a weird one, just look at the squid.

Bones Prove Evolution?-Has this crossover creature proven evolution? I think not. All it shows is senseless experimentation. It doesn't show survival of the fittest; it shows survival of the most bizarre.

No matter how you say it, this not having an opening and shooting the penis into the water doesn't sound like survival of the fittest, it sounds like someone having fun with genetics, especially when you add the highly advanced eyeball in an animal with not bones sometimes and with bones other times.

Stationary Animals Don't Fit-Besides the above, there is also the oyster. The oyster is not very mobile. It attaches itself to rocks and stays its whole life in one position; yet over 200 species of these "rock appendages" are found in Europe, Africa, North and South America. How could they cross the entire ocean and be distributed along all continents? To make things even more interesting, oysters of Europe are unisexual, but in America, they are double-sexed so we know that they don't mix with one another. How could one be derived from the other? There must have been some outside help. The simple answer might be that ancients simply liked oysters and made them the way they liked them.

Frog Eyeballs Don't Fit-If you are still not convinced that most animals are experimental rather than naturally selected or immediately created, let's look at the frog for a minute. I don't mean let's look at his head and say his head should be for an animal much bigger than he is. The thing that may show that it is a non-evolved, genetically experimented thing is its eyeballs, but it doesn't have great eyesight like the squid.

The frog swallows its food with its eyeballs.

Whenever it captures an animal in its mouth, it essentially squeezes the food down its throat by tightly closing its eyes and forcing the eyeball to push the food down. I have a hard time believing that God designed this anomaly and the "evolution" of eyeball swallowing doesn't make sense either. Where are the other eyeball swallowers? The ghost eye frog shown below even has a weird eye to boot.

Lizard Eyeballs Don't Fit-While we are on the subject of eyes and things inappropriate for evolution, we cannot leave out the Texas Horned Lizard. There's an evolved capability we all should have. His method for defense is to shoot his blood out of his eye. If it is sufficiently frightened it can squirt up 1/3 of its volume of blood out of pores next to its eye area according to researchers Middendorf and Sherbrooke. The graphic above shows the effect.

Plants Don't Fit-If these impossible evolutionary capabilities don't make you sit up and wonder, then what about the very simple change from animals to plants? How did plants evolve separately from animals; and for that matter, what is a plant anyway? What we call plants are, many times, more complex than our evolved animals friends, so even what came first the chicken or the eggplant has to also be questioned. Maybe at one time there was a significant distinction between the two, but, in many ways, the distinctive is no longer significant. This lack of separation in the face of major differences in genetic make-up strongly suggests "artificial" combination of characteristics.

- If you say it is characterized by having **roots**, then what about sponges, corals, sea-fans, sea-lilies, barnacles, zoophytes, mussels, sea-squirts, oysters and similar animals? Those animals have roots.

- If you said **green color**, then what about red and brown seaweed and mushrooms.

- If you said **chlorophyll**, then what about the euglena, volvox, bell-animalcule. Those animals all have chlorophyll while mushroom plants do not.

- If you said feed on **carbonic acid gas**, then what about the animal called bell-animalcule. That's exactly what it likes and mushrooms don't like it.

- If you said a plant has no **brain**, then how does a green bean find its way around a shaft to secure itself or flowers close at night or the Venus flytrap insect eating machine eat insects? On and on, we can go with instances showing plant "brain power" greater than some things classified as animals.

- If you said **lower order** of evolution, I certainly can show complex creatures that are called plants.

- If you said **red blood**, you would be wrong again as many animals do not have red blood.

- If you said **sex** you would be wrong again with all those stamens and pistils, and many animals do not use sex as a means to procreation. Many animals, on the other hand do not use sex for reproduction.

For those that do use sex, many forms of animals change from one sex to another yearly. Some change as they get older. Some are both male and female all the time.

I don't think that there is a distinction between the two separately discussed creatures and we should, probably, think of them both as animals until the separation can be completely determined. Oh by the way, all this evolving to make plants closer to animals and, at the same time, not changing to insure that animals and plants have distinctive differences has never been witnessed. It's another made up idea. Some of the same plants and animals that existed even during the Cretaceous period are found today—completely unevolved. It's almost as if modifications were not done by natural selection at all but, instead the changes were accomplished by willful and purposeful direct modification of DNA chains. One thing that shouldn't be in this book is sperm noses.

Sperm Noses seem odd- Few think about how basic the sense of smell really is. I know this has little to do with our story, but I thought you would like to know that German and US scientists have discovered a smell receptor "nose" molecule on the surface of human sperm cells, similar to those in the nose. The researchers found that sperm swim towards the smell of a substance called bourgeonal that is released by the ovum. They also found that another compound, called undecanal, blocks the effect of bourgeonal. So if the ovum get sprayed with undecanal, the sperm are not interested and no fertilization occurs and that brings us to hippopotamus.

Hippopotamus Sperm-Sorry for the sperm diversion, but I'm trying to show that the strange animal characteristics are not the result of evolution going haywire or God simply changing his mind and sperm noses might be one of the things integrated into our DNA by the experimenters.

Even if you take away the sperm nose idea, there is something comical about the fact that hippopotamus have the shortest sperm of any mammal, but this comedy isn't by chance. It also is most likely the result of Nephilimic science. The Nephilim were not creators, they were DNA recombiner hacks working willi-nilli without understanding the consequences of their changes to God's animals. Let's look at a really sad one called the whale. Rather than the sperm whale which somehow seems to fit here, I think the horrors of a baleen whale are much more drastic.

Making a Whale-Anak geneticists possibly started with a grouper but added DNA associated with a human brain which was attached to some of their Anak giantism. Not only did the fish grow, but it took on the characteristics of a mammal with a 10 pound brain [3 times as large as a normal human]. The arm and leg DNA was stripped away and finally the morbid scientist added that stupid baleen DNA so that the largest of all animals had to eat the tiniest shrimp in the ocean. We hear the moaning of whales all the time and think it is music, but possibly they cry as they see others eating real food or thinking about how some fantastic machine could be built and no arms to attempt anything. Then they just went too far as they made the whale unable to breathe in the water. The images below show the sad whale, his baleen, and his tiny food.

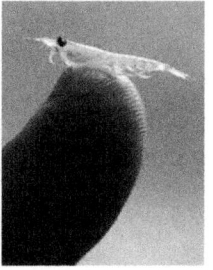

God hated what they were doing-Ancient texts simply tell us God hated what the Anak and the Cro-Magnon humans were doing so much he destroyed the Pleistocene with a mighty extinction and we are told almost all animals were abominations. One group of the modified animals that were technically abominations were the various primates. The Anak actually improved the early apes, but they never got them to where they could talk or reliably take commands.

Timeline That Fits

The following timeline shows a logical progression of key elements as dated by conventional means and established by artifacts left from the specific events. I know it's not the timeline you are used to, but it fits the evidence. I know new timing data suggests this timeline can be compressed, but let's use the "accepted" timing for this overview.

Years Ago	Description
600,000	Tiny animals appeared by some means in Cambrian
400,000	Trilobites and similar animals appeared in Permian
300,000	Giant Humans appear by the end of Triassic
200,000	Highly civilized humans in Jurassic
150,000	Dinosaurs and humans live together on earth during the Cretaceous.
120,000	Large Dinosaurs become extinct along with most animals. Anak Humans survive the extinction
110,000	Anak make the Proconsul [first Ape]
100,000	Australopithicus [part ape part man]
90,000	Homo-Erectus man and Gigantopithicus Ape-man
70,000	Gorilla ape, Meganthropus Ape-man, Neanderthal man [slightly larger brain than modern man]
40,000	Cro-Magnon. Different than most mammals. He has no penis bone and his brain is larger than Neanderthal's.
80,000	
10,000	Worldwide flood almost all animals die a few species survive on boats during Pleistocene Extinction.
5,000	Massive war, Ape-men, and Chimpanzee mutations and many new races of men.
Over the last 5,000	Essentially no new animals evolve

For this timeline to work, some type of genetic manipulation had to have occurred. Hopefully by now you are beginning to believe the people of this time had the scientists to accomplish they types of things our biologists are doing today---messing up animals. In the "general animal" world, these modifications were not done by smart sperm determining how the DNA strings should be organized. Without "outside" help, the changes required for evolution would never occur **with enough quantity** to become viable fro procreation.

Consensus of Evolution

Here we go. How can anyone say uncontrolled evolution doesn't work? Are all the consensus scientists and teachers stupid? Of course not, but many are held captives by previous beliefs or what I call consensus of peers as scientist never want to purposely say some peer is an idiot, so things fester for years. I wrote a whole book of this consensus problem. For years scientists touted how Heroine would cure everything. Then they switched to radioactive Radium as a cure-all. Even after people got sick and died, the community stuck together. When Molescopy was the craze, many went to doctors to find out about their moles; and when Phrenology came along we had the same issue. Now consensus scientists are still clinging to climate change being caused by people, but none of this means scientists are stupid nor does it mean they are correct just because there is consensus. I need to back up here and readdress the evolution issue as I brought up a little previously. Because we need to recognize that undirected evolution is not what we have evidence of today. What we have evidence of is experimentation up until about 5 thousand years ago and then nothing. No experimentation and generally no modifications. If we assume that God would not need to experiment, and that the natural selection concept doesn't support reduced capability outcomes, we must consider ancient human manipulation during many phases of our earth's history.

Early Evolution-Ancient texts from around the world talk about a very ancient time when the people of earth battled with the people of the heavens. By general comparison, this ancient war occurred about 100 thousand years ago. While we have little concrete evidence of this or any of the other major wars what we do find is that the civilization level of mankind seems to ebb and flow. During an ancient time his capabilities were highly advanced and a few hundred years later, all the advancements seem to disappear as if mankind had to start over, just as you would expect from a major catastrophe.

Evidence suggests that before the heaven wars, the ancient humans realized that this "evolution" had its problems. Just about the time when reasonable creatures were made, some major catastrophe would destroy everything and they would have to start from scratch. Soon the inhabitants must have realized that they should keep samples of the creatures so that they could quickly revive the creatures that were lost by each successive extinction period.

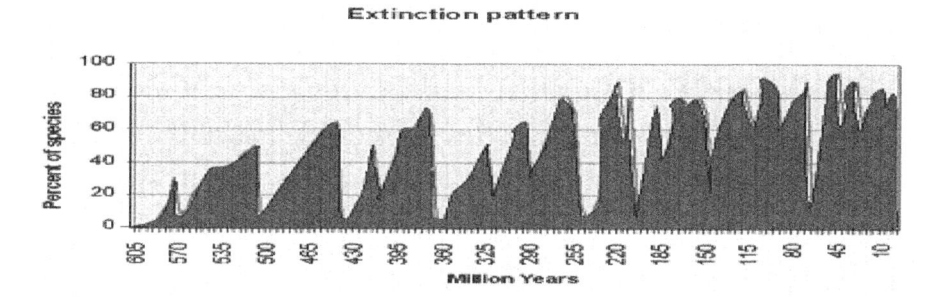

Extinction pattern

While the recoveries of animals after each of the later extinctions make no sense, I think looking as families of animals rather than species may show it better and bring out something important. I though a couple of charts will help you. First off, there is no question that a level of evolution occurs but in order for modifications to not push a species further and further into disorder [Law of Entropy], some outsider MUST modify the chain of events to assure advancement of a species rather than the slow destruction of entropy. There is little doubt the Anak people had violated the laws of God by "miscreating" animals all over the place.

Some of the miscreated were considered human. Most of the miscreating was just biologists having fun; completely unconcerned about the outcome. If you look in *"Encyclopedia Britannica"*, they present the first chart shown next as the development of animals and when they occurred. Essentially they stated that for millions of years there was about 500 different families of animals. Even extinctions had almost no effect on the families of animals.

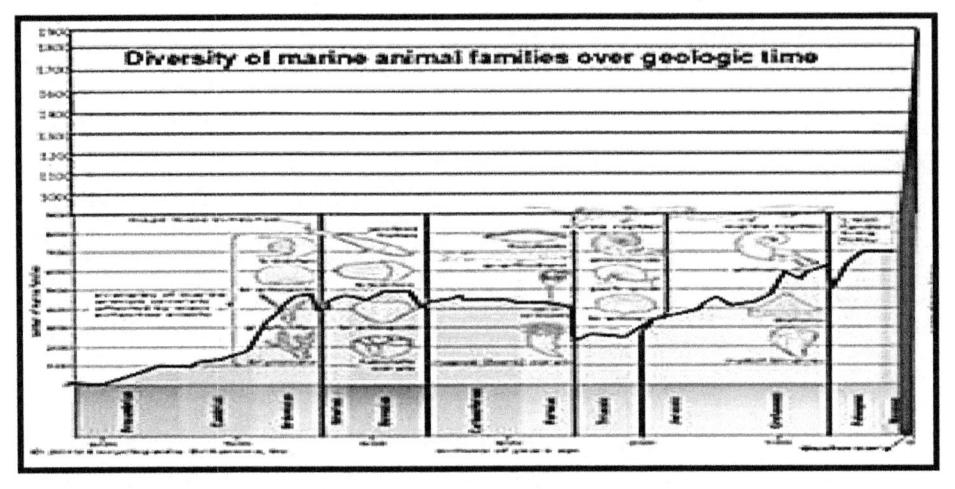

Diversity of marine animal families over geologic time

About 40 thousand years ago the encyclopedia tells us BAM 1600 families of animals miraculously appeared in the blink of an eye.

Change Timing- We need to look at the new timing method because nuclear decay was so wrong. I modified the chart using the new timing. Guess what? We now have 500 families of animals over hundreds of thousands of years and then BAM! 1600 almost overnight as if some massive group of genetic engineers were engineering away just like we are starting to do today, but the slope doesn't go to infinity. There can be little question about the ANAK miscreating all types of animals including the remanufacture of dinosaurs and the manipulation of Apes and humans.

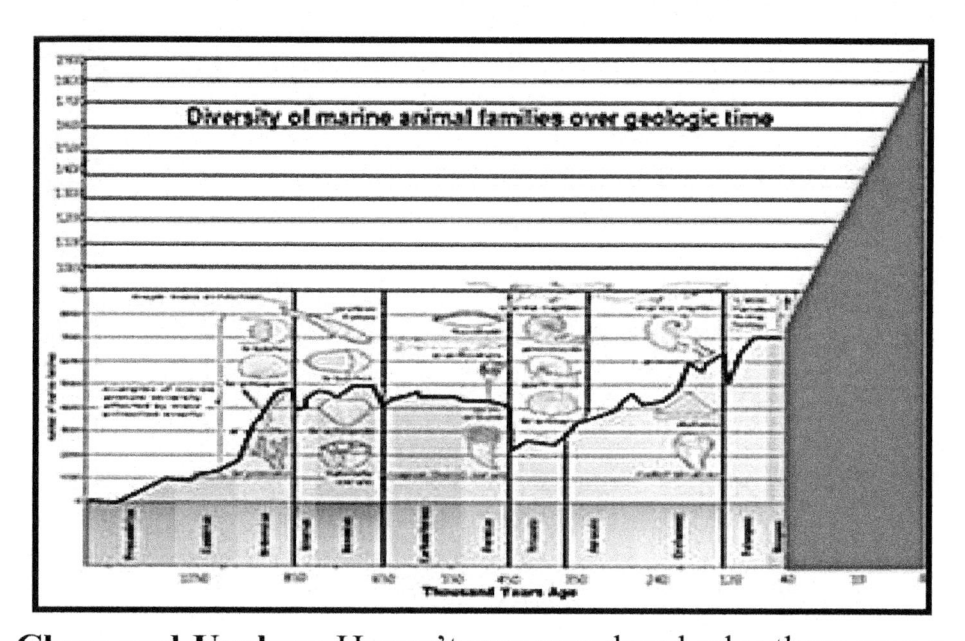

Diversity of marine animal families over geologic time

Clean and Unclean-Haven't you wondered why there was a distinction between clean and unclean/abominable animals? The clean animals would most likely have been those created by God, while the abominable ones would have been modified and left unsuitable for Adamic humans to eat or associate with. Here is what various ancient Jewish texts had to say about the creation of clean animals. Later we will investigate the whole unclean thing. Notice that even these *"clean" creatures came from the earth rather than from God's original creation.* For those who are mad that I would suggest that most animals are abominations, let me tell you that the word abomination and unclean are the same word in Hebrew. It appears, in the verses below, that genetic modification was usually done with the acknowledgement of God.

Genesis 1:24-30- *And heavenly ones said, Let "**the Earth**" bring forth the living creature after his kind, cattle, and creeping thing, and beast of the Earth after his kind. [**I assume the term "earth made the animals" really is "Nephilim or Anak made the animals" as they were the rulers of the earth at that time.**]*

***Book of Abraham 4:24**-The gods prepared <u>the Earth</u> to bring forth the living things. - and the gods organized **the Earth** to bring forth the beasts. [**This suggests that someone on the earth was instrumental in the creation of the beasts of the earth.**]*

***II Esdras 6:48**-On the 6th day you ordered <u>the Earth</u> to produce for you cattle, wild beasts, and creeping things.*

My personal belief is that God helping you manipulate DNA would result in perfect animals, so some of the genetics that was practiced was, more than likely, done without his oversight when Moses indicated God "Rested" and he simply watched what happened "*Genesis 2:1*". That is where the abominable animals come in. Scientists looked around and found all sorts of strange animals and tried to piece together a crazy story that would put together all the mistakes that were made during the genetic experiments but they haven't found a workable solution to date.

Possible Evolution-Some say there are many, many things that show evolution and survival of the fittest controls history. Certainly there is a level of change in species, but when it comes down to it, cross species changes and even interspecies oddities cannot be answered by evolution alone. Something else was going on and Apes were a frequent receiver of this "else".

Experiments on Animals

Whether the Angels evolved from the Ancient Humans [Titans] or were a separate creation doesn't matter to this history very much, but at some time Angels appeared on the scene after the ancient humans. They lived without causing trouble for a while, but after a very long time on Earth many of the angels learned how to accomplish genetic manipulation on the animal life just like their predecessors, the ancient humans had. This whole manipulation concept should not be difficult to believe because our current version of humans have only been looking into this possibility for a very short time and already have had major breakthroughs in genetics.

Italian, UK, and Clone Miracles-In Italy, scientists have learned how to change the chromosome pattern in a pig so that a human heart will be generated instead of its normal heart. In the UK they are genetically mutating the brain of a rat to make him smart, and there is no telling how many clones that have been generated to support the growth of science. Just think how good we would be at manipulating animal genetics if we spent hundreds of thousands of years as did the ancient humans and the angels. With genetic manipulations there came unusual genetic similarities and disassociations which can be traced. Today we know this anomaly of our genetic code as the alien genes.

Alien Genes-This section is concerning alien genes that have been found in humans and reported in "Nature" Magazine. It seems that scientists now can determine the ancestors of animals by looking at the genetic patterns. With 140 thousand genes, the number of ancestors of humans is large, but scientists are puzzled by 223 of the genes that have NO apparent ancestor bond. This means that these scientists believe that some unknown creature was partially responsible for the genetic makeup of modern humans. Of course, you should know by now that the aliens that these scientists have discovered were, more than likely, the Nephilim. Much of the manipulation was not done with the approval or oversight of the Creator God and that's where many of the problems arose. It is not surprising that, during this time, huge creatures, like the thousands of types of dinosaurs, were created as they tested the limits of this new toy we call genetics. Speaking of genetics, we must review the story of human creation as told by the ancient people of Mongolia.

Mongolian Creation of Man

God created a man and woman out of clay. Their entire bodies were covered with a layer of fur. This was during a time when the seas were still rising. He went to get some "everlasting life water" and ordered a dog and cat to watch over his new creations. The devil gave the animals some milk to distract them while <u>he urinated all over the humans</u>. God was angry with the dog and cat for not caring for the humans. As punishment God made the cat lick off all the hair from the human body except for the area around the groin and under the arms. After each lick, God placed the fur that was taken away and placed it on the identical area of the disobedient dog.

If you notice, a dog doesn't have much hair around its groin and armpits, while a human is exactly the opposite [quite un evolutionary if you ask me.] Maybe they were on to something and the evolution believing, science community is mistaken. Speaking of mistakes, just like the genetic mistakes we have today and those we will surely have in the near future as we get better at this genetics thing--- the ancients had many MISTAKES.

Greek Mistakes-The Greeks were great to bring out a wide variety of genetically manipulated beings that were mistakish. One of the creatures produced could have been similar to the Greek Centaur or the flying horse as shown below.

The unicorn, identified in many pieces of literature could have also been one of the mistakes made by the genetic mutators. Certainly these creatures could be imaginary, but usually when similar stories are told by different people and similar creatures are discussed that are associated with different regions, the likelihood of there being truth somewhere in the stories goes up. The flying horse and partial man/animal creatures are seen everywhere in ancient texts and verbal histories. We need to get at that kernel of truth.

Aye Aye Evolution

The cute little Aye Aye has a much "evolved" appendage. Its evolved member is its middle finger. You see, the Aye Aye likes termites and this delicacy lives deep inside trees. Only small holes give their position away and that's where the old Aye Aye's finger comes in. Its middle finger is long and skinny. I don't mean slightly long, I mean tremendous. It looks like it is trying to make nasty signs with its hands, but the middle finger can also fit down into the tree holes and pull out termites. Possibly, aye ayes in the olden days that didn't have the long finger so most just died because the termites were unreachable, but maybe the long finger was a mistake and Aye-ayes have "evolved to use the stupid thing.

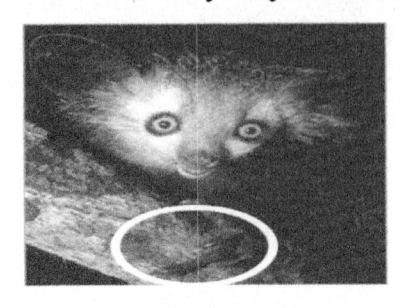

The Sumerians drew and wrote about creatures that were part man part fish or part lion, or part eagle. Greeks had the Cyclops [a one eyed monster], and many more. Many societies had part snake part men creatures. The Egyptians and Greeks had the Sphinx. Above right is an axe head from Bactrian in central Asia. The man in the middle has 2 bird heads and the lion has wings. I know that's not normal, but during this time, there were probably a lot of weird things walking, crawling, or flying around. Some of the monsters were fictitious, but many, I believe, were actual creatures that were manufactured to be as indicated in the ancient texts. We are told the whole genetic manipulation thing angered God. The ancient Jewish book of Enoch possibly said it better than other ancient histories. Let's read the following warnings.

Enoch I 7:5- *And they began to sin with birds and with animals and with reptiles, and with fish.* [This did not mean that the Nephilim had sex with fish. This is talking about manipulation of species]

Unicorn-One of the creatures that probably was made during this time is the unicorn. The Bible talks about how powerful it was and, in ancient Mohen jo Daro, pictures were drawn of this creature. From the looks of it, it must have been a cross between a horse, a cow, and a goat. There aren't any unicorns alive today, but even after the flood, they were talked about and drawings were created which showed them. [Note the yoke on the Mohenjo-Daro version of the unicorn. It suggests that they used domesticated "unicorn power".]

Here are some of the descriptions of the unicorn from the Bible that suggest a manmade creation. .

Numbers 23:22*- God brought them out of Egypt; he hath as it were the strength of a **unicorn**.*

Psalms 92:10*- But my horn shalt thou exalt like the horn of a **unicorn**: I shall be anointed with fresh oil.*

Numbers 24:8*- God brought him forth out of Egypt; he hath as it were the strength of a **unicorn**:*

Other Genetic Mutants

Here are some other mutants we may already be familiar with including the Centaur, Medusa the Gorgon, the Sphinx, Typhus, the Dragon, Satyrs, and even an inverted sphinx. The list of mutated beings was probably unbelievable and endless. Many could have been REAL. Just because none of the creatures are alive today does not necessarily mean they didn't live before the flood or even afterwards for that matter. The next collage simply shows a few of the hundreds of "in between" animals that were "made" sometime between 40 thousand and 5 thousand years ago.

Inverted Sphinx-The 35 thousand year old German carving on Ivory shown above to the right is half lion half human, but unlike the sphinx, the head part is the lion part.

Egyptian Inverted Sphinx-Next to it, the Egyptians remembered the same reverse sphinx. This was the goddess of pleasure, Bast.

Satyrs-We find satyrs everywhere. These also could have been Cherubimic Nephilim or genetic mistakes. Below are Biblical and Greek mythological examples, but one thing is certain; they are popular creatures.

Greek Satyr-Satyrs may have been one of the mistakes of the genetic breeding programs. This 16th century painting shows the ½ goat- ½ human animals in action. His favorite pastime was sex.

Gnostic Texts

Nag Hammadi Creation Text- *God was filled with anger and said " You are mistaken, Samael, there is an immortal man of light that has been in existence before you, and who will appear <u>amid the creatures you have made</u>, and will trample you, and you will descend to the abyss--- [then he and his followers] made a great war in the seven heavens.*

Besides making Apes, creatures that were made and remade were dinosaurs or massive animals. After all, bigger shows more skill in genetics. One remade dinosaur was called the dragon.

We know of at least 130 of these flying dragons that filled the sky with wingspans of 23 feet and always hungry, for some reason Anak remade these things. We call the Pterosaurs, buy in the old days they didn't make up fancy names.

Mutant Dragons

Here is some more initially, unbelievable information that appears to show genetic manipulation. In fact, because the last chapter of the book of Daniel discussed the destruction of a dragon, the chapters containing the dragon were removed from the Bible in 1827. The "inappropriate chapters", typically called "Bel and the Dragon", had to be removed before the remaining chapters of the book were allowed to remain as part of the current Bible. Even though we choose not to believe these were actual creatures, the ancients knew of them and feared them.

Again and again the ancient people went to their stash of genetic components that made up animals and re-made the creatures as they had done many time before. We are probably at the middle of the Tertiary period. During this fateful time, some of the beasts were being genetically manipulated to fight against the heavenly host, according to the Sumerian, Greek, and Jewish texts. God, of course, created the creatures initially, but the angels modified them relentlessly and sometimes with horrifying results. This genetic manipulation became commonplace, but even with some pretty amazing creatures, the rebels lost a war between rebel "angels" and those called the heaven host. Being turned into humans didn't teach the losers anything as they immediately began designing new creatures and teaching the other humans about the wonders of changing species. We can read about the Nephilimic genetic studies in ancient Jewish, Hittite, Sumerian, Chinese, Indian, Greek, and just about every text from around the world.

The Hittite's dragon, Illuyankas.-According to the Bible, the Dragon fought in the war against heaven. The Bible says people worshipped it like a god. In Sumerian texts, the Annunaki [angels] designed the dragon especially for fighting in the Heaven Wars. The Sumerian Dragon was given a "Halo" so that it could be a major participant in the war and be like a god. Although we may not be sure what a halo is really good for, we can be pretty certain that it was something significant and different than that had by all other animals except for the angels. The Dragon was designed to be very powerful and it was no unthinking beast, as we sometimes believe. It was able to talk, according to Biblical testimony, and also work miracles. It was also able to transfer to other monsters some of these marvelous powers. The Bible also says it had as many as 7 heads just like the dragons that were described in Hittite history, Chinese legend, and Greek mythology.

Dragons Fight-The blight on man of the Dragon is not over. According to many historical references, one of the dragons will participate in the future war with heaven. Here are some excerpts found in ancient texts.

Sumerian Creation Epic-*And Taimat [depiction of Satan] said, Let us make monsters that they may go out and do battle. Hubur [one of the rebel angels] arose. She bore monsters-Serpents, sharp of tooth, long of fangs. She crowned them with* **halos** *and made them as Gods- The mighty creatures of Hubur were slain.* [They were slain while participating in the heaven wars.]

Greek Mythology- *In those stories Gaia [Satan], after the defeat of her Giants, created* **[genetically manipulated]** *Typhon [half serpent/ half man] to take revenge on the gods.* [This may have been a reference to the creation of the Dragon for use in the Heaven War.]

Biblical References

Isaiah 14-Satyrs *shall dance and the wild beasts of* **the islands** *shall cry in their desolate houses, and* **dragons** *in their pleasant* **palaces** *[Why would dragons be in palaces unless they were like angels and rulers during an ancient time?]*

Psalm 74: 13-14-Thou didst divide the sea by thy strength: thou brakest the heads of the **dragons** *in the waters. Thou brakest the heads of* **leviathan** *in pieces, and gavest him to be meat to the people inhabiting the wilderness.* [This is possibly indicates that the Leviathan and Dragon were the same genetically bred thing.]

Sumerian Dragons

From the Sumerian, Turkish, Egyptian, Norse, and Persian depictions, it is clear that the dragons fought in the first heaven war.

Asag- This Sumerian Dragon stole the tablets of Destiny but they were recovered before the world was changed.

Tiamat- This Babylonian Dragon tried to take over heaven. She spawned eleven monsters to help her make war.

Persian Dragons

Azhi Dahaki- This **three-headed** Persian Dragon was the Father of Lies and created Azhi Dahaki to rid the world of righteousness by extinguishing the light of a sacred flame known as The Divine Glory. He was imprisoned on Mount Demavend. It is believed that at the end of the world, the dragon will be freed and he will devour one third of all men and animals before finally being defeated. [This is very close to the Revelation story of the final battle, isn't it?]

Hittite Dragon-*Illuyankas*-This Hittite Dragon tried to take over heaven and was killed by the storm-god.

Canaanite Dragon- *Yam-nahar-* This Canaanite, seven headed, sea Dragon was destroyed by the young god Baal.

Egyptian Dragons- *Apophis* -This Egyptian sea-serpent/dragon attempted to destroy the sun-god Atum-Ra.

Greek Dragons- *Ladon-* This Greek Dragon was the guardian of the golden apples and was slain by Hercules.

Central American Dragons- *Quetzalcoatl-* This Toltec Dragon was a benign serpent as the bringer of light to his people and sometimes he adopted human form.

Chinese Dragons- *Dragon Kings-*fought wars in the skies with fantastic weapons according to Chinese tradition.

Northern European Dragons

*Nidhogg-*This Norse Dragon continuously tried to destroy the universe.

Firedrake – This Norse Dragon fought Beowulf in his final battle and the hero died of his wounds.

Norse Dragon- Once he lived as a giant, but the dwarfs transformed their greatest Dragon.

Modern Sightings

Below may have been a recent find s from the 19th and 20th centuries. Newspapers showed the things and discussed sightings.

Some were lucky enough to get very close to these ½ grown dragons. Sometimes the images are faked, but the quantity makes us wonder. The upper right image has been debunked, but others still question how many of the Anak's 130 dragons may have lived through the Pleistocene extinction.

New Dinosaurs

That brings us to "fresh" dinosaur skin and tissue. Some try simply say dinosaurs didn't die until 20 thousand years ago. Bah Humbug! [Sorry for the outburst!] That being said some dinosaurs/ dragons did not die at the end of the Cretaceous or they would all be fossilized. As just mentioned there was a war just before the end of the Pleistocene, 10 thousand years ago, which places the second destruction of Dinosaurs during the time of the preflood Cro-Magnon people. From Sumerian and other texts, we are told, dinosaurs were remade during the war. I don't know what they used them for, but we are starting to find these animals all over, so don't discount the obvious. Some were even remade after the massive worldwide flood that marked the Pleistocene Extinction as seen in post flood artifacts. Here is what we know. Soft tissue [un-fossilized stuff] inside dinosaur bones has been found and more and more finds are being seen each year. This can only mean the dinosaurs were alive until recent times. Some of the many finds are shown below.

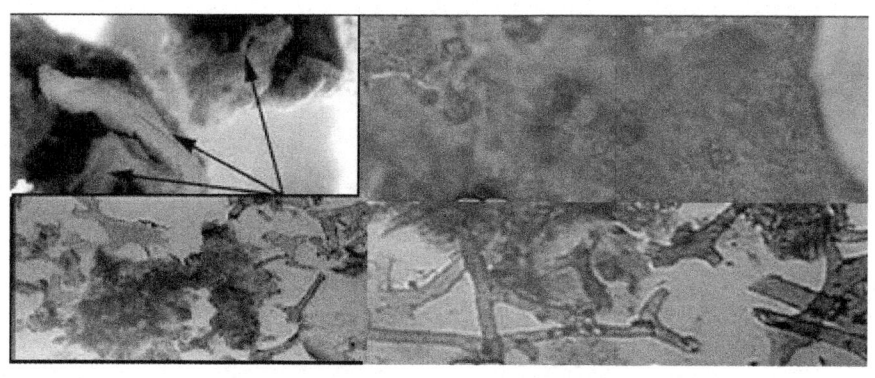

Less than 50 Thousand Years Old

While the geologists were squabbling, there has been pretty much consensus that soft tissues must be less than 50 thousand years old. Most say if the insides are less than 50 thousand years old the dinosaur that died must have lived less than 50 thousand years ago. They have been finding soft tissue since 2007 and more continues. As of April 2014 researchers have discovered flexible and transparent blood vessels, red blood cells, many various proteins including the microtubule building block tubulin, collagen, the cytoskeleton component actin, and hemoglobin, bone maintenance osteocyte cells, and powerful evidence for DNA. Blood vessels from a T-Rex are shown below.

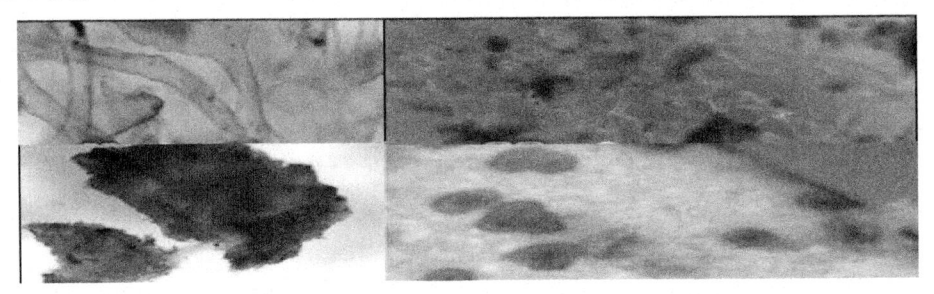

The list of dinosaurs that were, apparently remade during the Pleistocene keeps growing and now includes <u>Hadrosaur, titanosaurs, mosasaur, Triceratops, Lufengosaurs, T. Rex, ornithomimosaur, and Archaeopteryx.</u>

Triceratops and Hadrosaur bones from Montana were tested for Carbon 14 two different dating labs both said that the triceratops registered an average of 31,000 radiocarbon years and 23,000 years was the date for the Hadrosaur. Some researchers cut open a number of T-Rex bones and found masses of soft material that had not fossilized yet. Meaning the animal was less than 50,000 years old. The scientific community went berserk. This was a lie; this was a mistake; this was an anomaly. Soon all the back pointing was of no use as more and more finds showed the same thing. Some T-

Rexes lived well past the time of the reported extinction. An example of the elastic material is shown below.

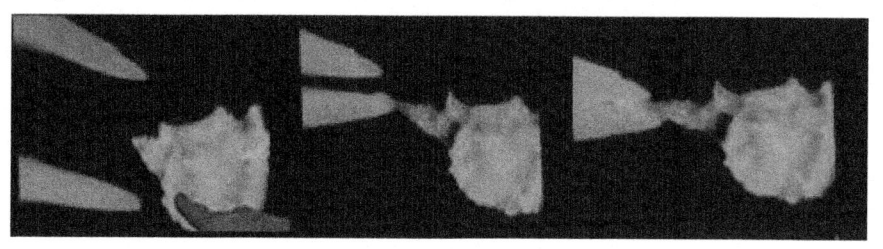

Young Smilodon

Recent radiocarbon dating done <u>on collagen</u> that was taken from " femur bones" of twelve extinct saber tooth tigers, from the LeBrea Tar Pits of Los Angeles California ranged from 12,650 to 28,000 years before the present. Oops!!!

I thought everything died during the great extinction!!!

There is no question that the K-T chalk barrier marks a massive extinction at the end of the Cretaceous. The T-Rex, Triceratops, Hadrosaur, Lufengosaurs, Ornithomimosaur, Mosasaur, Titanosaurs, and Archaeopteryx would have been on the list of extinction receivers. The <u>new evidence is almost irrefutable, so something happened? These animals were re-manufactured</u> before the great extinction period that marks the Pleistocene Extinction. It would have been easy to reestablish any of the dinosaurs desired if DNA had been stored or if viable DNA was found on dead animals of that time and geneticists were just slightly better than today. If they made dinosaurs, it would have been easy to make all sorts of apes. Here are some of more examples besides "Generations of Adam", and "Enoch" presented before. the examples of what was said about the making of animals. Just about everywhere you look we find that animals were genetically modified including Dinosaurs. Some may have even been regenerated after the worldwide flood.

Jubilees 4:8- *And lawlessness increased on the earth and <u>all flesh corrupted its way, alike men and cattle and beasts and birds and everything that walks on the earth -all of them corrupted their ways and their orders</u>,*

Jubilees-7:3- *And after this [The war] they <u>sinned against the beasts and birds</u>.* [There are two ways to sin against beasts- sex and genetic manipulation. The corrupted animals were known as <u>"unclean"</u> monsters. All reptiles were in this unclean animal list.]

II Enoch 59:5-6- *But whosoever kills a beast without wounds, kills his own soul and defiles his flesh. <u>And he who does any beast any injury whatsoever, in secret, it is evil practice, and he defiles his own soul</u>.* [The killing and injury done in secret was not killing animals for food, it was, most likely, genetic manipulation]

Book of Creation- *and who will appear <u>amid the creatures you [Satan and the Nephilim]have made</u>, and will trample you, and you will descend to the abyss--- then he and his followers <u>made a great war</u> .* [Like the Sumerian version, Satan and his cohorts designed animal monsters to fight in another Heaven War. Many of the monsters he designed were huge dinosaurs.]

Book of Naphtali 1:25-26- *The Gentiles went astray, and forsook the Lord and <u>changed their order</u>, and obeyed stocks and stones, spirits of deceit—become not as <u>Sodom, which changed the order of nature</u>.* [Not only does it indicate that the watchers or angels and gentiles practiced genetic manipulation, but also that the practice was the major cause for the flood. If you wondered why Sodom went up in smoke in the Bible, this verse indicates they were changing the order of nature-----beginning to change animals.]

Book of Creation-*Samael [Satan] said," I have no need for anyone-it is I who am God, and there is no other one that* *exists from me"---Pisitis [**God**] was filled with anger and said " You are mistaken, Samael, there is an immortal man of light that has been in existence before you, and who will appear **amid the creatures you have made**, and will trample you, and you will descend to the abyss--- then he and his followers made a great war in the seven heavens.* [Like the Sumerian version, Satan and his cohorts designed animal monsters to fight in a War. Many of the monsters he designed were huge dinosaurs.]

You can't tell while you are reading this, but a little tear has welled up in my eye as I think about how the children are being taught the survival of the fittest evolutionary process as a fact of science, when there is no substantial evidence about its truth. Anyway; Genetic engineering was rampant during the Pleistocene. The Bible describes Clean and abominable/unclean animals to separate manufactured or reconstructed from natural animals. If they were making all these, you have to believe ape's would have been high on their list as it was like making man. Today we are told scientists have made animals that are as much as 30% human with almost human hearts, ears, skin, and all types of things recovered from the unfortunate bastardized animals. Below shows the famous featherless chicken, mouse with a human ear, and the many parts of pigs now be experimented on to fix humans. We will look at this later.

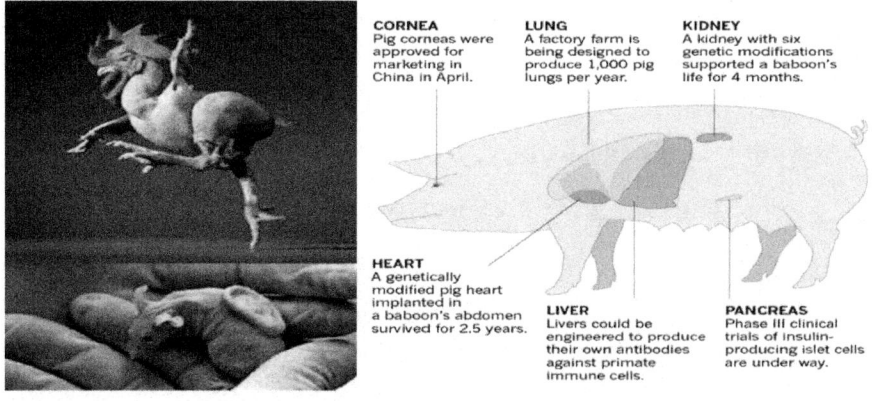

CORNEA
Pig corneas were approved for marketing in China in April.

LUNG
A factory farm is being designed to produce 1,000 pig lungs per year.

KIDNEY
A kidney with six genetic modifications supported a baboon's life for 4 months.

HEART
A genetically modified pig heart implanted in a baboon's abdomen survived for 2.5 years.

LIVER
Livers could be engineered to produce their own antibodies against primate immune cells.

PANCREAS
Phase III clinical trials of insulin-producing islet cells are under way.

War and Mutation

War broke out just before the end of the Pleistocene and many lives were lost, but the thing important about apes during this time is that nuclear materials were used and we can believe the fallout was a major reason for Man changing so much before heading into the Holocene Age. Before the ware there were very few major mutations of the Cro-Magnon based humans on the earth and most of the other breeds had all but been eliminated. All of a sudden there were 9 major mutations. Besides the massive mutations 5 thousand years ago, these would be the worst changes in our DNA up until this time. We can believe apes had a similar fate.

9 Major Mutations

Today everything you hear about is DNA and mutation so let's track Apes with it as well. I mentioned that Chimpanzees had fewer major mutations in their DNA than modern humans. This is the major factor for determining Chimpanzees come from humans, but it is not that simple as mutations are not linearly homogenous. Almost all mutations ether occurred 10 thousand years ago [just before the Pleistocene Extinction] or 5 thousand years ago [during the Bharata War]. Let me show you what I mean.

Pleistocene Extinction Mutation

While the human beginning is much older that the 10 thousand year date, DNA Haplogrouping researchers study human characteristic to match DNA mutation and build timelines of races. Just before or during the Pleistocene

Extinction we find 10 brand new RACES of humans. Haplogroups shorthand places a letter by these major mutations. The following are the "Pleistocene Extinction" mutational Races of humans.

- C= Negroid
- E= Eastern Nubian
- G= Proto Europe
- H= Proto Afghan
- I = Proto Greek
- N= Proto Russian
- O= Proto Oriental
- K= Proto Asian
- J= Proto Egyptian
- F= Cro-Magnon

One day they were all the same and the next day all these variations, somehow happened. Let me stop here just a minute, while I am presenting the probability that chimpanzees mutated after the Bharata War, I think it is reasonable to describe some primate DNA. As shown below it has been determined that the genetic difference between Bonobo and Chimps is about the same as that of the Neanderthal-man and much less than the Denisovan-man who both were considered variants of the Pleistocene Age. This was simply done by counting the number of differences in a DNA chain.

Homo-Genus	Selected DNA Nucleotide sequence	Genetic Distance to CRS
CRS (modern standard)	c c t c g c a c c t c a a c t a a c c t c t t t t t	-
Bonobo	. . . c . . . . . . a g . . c c c t . . a . c c c .	>11
Chimps	. . . . . t g . . . . c g . . c t . t . t . c . c .	>10
Feldhofer Neanderthal	. t . . . t . . . . . . g . c . . t . . . . c . .	6
Denisova Cave	a - c t - a - a - c a c t a g - c g g a - - c g a c	>19

Let me show you another sequence [not the same as above] to show how very close we are to these modified humans.

```
Human:  G-C-C-G-A-T- A-A-G-C-A-C
        | | | | |    | | | | | |
Chimp:  G-C-C-G-A-G-A-A-G-C-A-C
```

I think I need to show one more example which combines the Orangutan, Gorilla, Chimpanzee and modern man. What we find is that just looking at the sequences shows the Orangutan and gorilla "dark and light spots" [technical jargon] are substantially different and the sequences are different lengths showing more or fewer Genes in a string. All these are signs of more ancient adaptation or both the Orangutan and Gorilla.

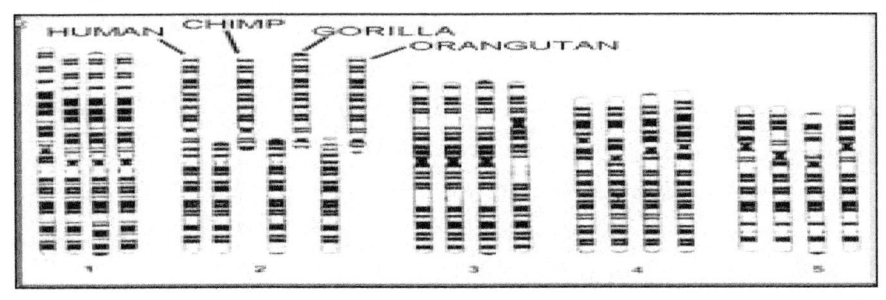

Mutation Oddness

Interestingly, researchers found male chimpanzees pass on twice as many mutations when compared to modern humans. While this is well known, no one has come up with a logical reason. Let me provide a few possibilities here.

- Human chromosomes are more protected [not likely]

- Chimpanzee do things that help chromosome mutate [not likely]

- Chimpanzee chromosomes are not natural and they are mutating more to restructure themselves back to "normal".

Chimpanzee mutation rates indicate a more unstable DNA Structure.

Size Shows a Similarity

Sorry for this short section, but I can't help it. Humans claim to have the largest penises of the apes, while the earlier apes had tiny appendages the chimpanzee and bonobo both have ones nearly as long as humans [over twice as long as Orangutans and Gorillas]. Chimpanzees use their excited devices for show to females a larger penis would provide a better display. Some humans have a similar tact, but they go to jail.

Chimpanzee   Human

There are 2 unusual differences. The diagram to the left shows a characteristic slope of a chimpanzee penis while the one on the right shows a similar organ on a human. For those upset with human anatomy, just put your finger over the right one and read on. There is nothing implied by shape, I am only showing that chimpanzee penis structure is different. The second difference is that humans have lost their penis bone [Baculum] and chimpanzees still have a small piece of one. The chart below shows that while a chimpanzee has a penis twice as large as a gorilla, its baculum or penis bone is half the size as shown in the chart. The image is of a gorilla baculum. These are very hard to get and it certainly will make the gorilla mad so do try to EVER get one of these things. The smaller the baculum the more human a primate becomes.

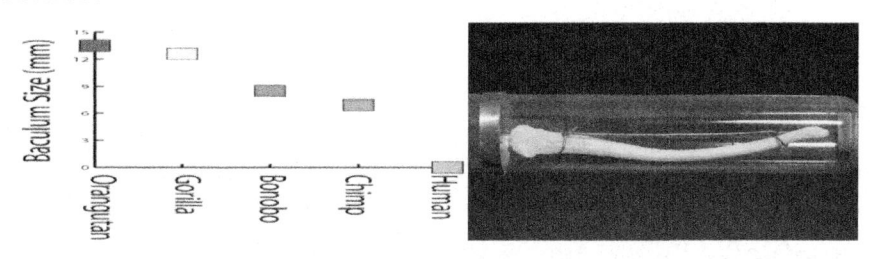

Chimpanzees display excited penises often to attract potential female mating partners. Unfortunately I have no answers about this, but that there is a large difference between Chimps and the other apes which help us understand about its close union with humans.

What Was Adam's Rib?

It could be that the "mutation" that established Cro-Magnon or modern humans caused a tiny difference that is well known and it may, very well, have been described in the Genesis history of the Bible. Because almost all male mammals have a penis bone [Baculum] and humans don't, one wonders just how this strange anomaly happened and it may help us understand something about the ancestry of humans and why our DNA changed to eliminate this structure over the last few years. We are hit with that odd statement again; later Cro-Magnon had no penis bone, but Chimpanzees do. The bones seem to be for increase in sensation, faster response, and longer copulation. Another theory is that monogamous mammals began to not require such a thing and it eventually disappeared so it is a good indication of evolution through non-reinforced mutation, but there might be another reason called the Tsala.

***Genesis 2:21-23-**So the LORD God caused a deep sleep to fall upon the man, and he slept; then <u>He took his "Tsala" [sometimes translated as "rib"]</u> and closed up the flesh at that place. The LORD God fashioned into a woman the "Tsala" which He had taken from the man, and brought her to the man. The man said, "This is now bone of my bones, and flesh of my flesh; She shall be called Woman, because she was taken out of Man."*

Notice I didn't say rib, but left the Hebrew transliterative form. In almost all cases, this word is **translated as "stumble", "side as side of a wall"**, or my favorite

"support structure". I don't know about you, but I can't see RIB as a supporting structure.

Certainly, God could have taken away one of the Ribs from men and we would have one less, but typically a rib is not associated with regeneration or reproduction.

There is a probability that the word could have been translated "Baculum" as no men have had these things since. Notice God never returned the bone to Adam. From this, we might believe that at some time, a vestigial Baculum will be found with Neanderthal remains as there is a good probability that Neanderthal was before Cro-Magnon. By the way, when Moses' book was being translated, there is no way they could have said penis bone as there simply was no understanding of such a thing beyond what Moses might have known somehow. For those not intimately aware of Baculum a few are shown in the next collage. The one to the left is from a proud walrus.

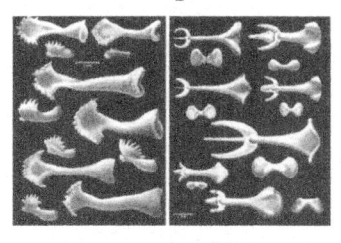

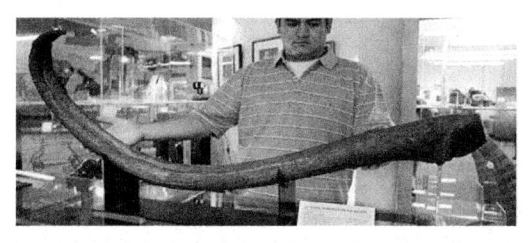

As man got larger his Baculum got smaller. We can believe Australopithecus had the bone. Habilis, and Erectus would have had a smaller one and the 4th one had none at all. For Apes it was similar. As the ape evolved, the baculum got smaller. Sorry for the strange section, let's get back on track.

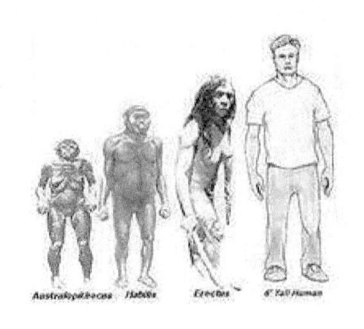

Please do not believe all humans walked out of Africa as a huge clump of different races. It did not happen that way. Yes, Homo-Erectus did have a large brow like many apes and most likely was the backdrop donor form many of the ape experiments, but the idea that there is a continuous progression of evolutionary characteristics of Apes that show so smooth progression is not true. Orangutan appeared; Gorilla simply appeared, and Chimpanzees appeared one day with substantial changes in their DNA. No matter if you believe these conclusions or not, the fact is that the "present human design" is **not** an offshoot design from the apes or other mammals. It also should be recognized that Apes have no evolution pattern and certainly they must have been manufactured randomly by some outside force. To this I say, "Researchers should not be looking at the width of the human brow to that of an ape or the minor pelvis design modifications. They should look at the brain, the penis, and DNA. We should recognize that the designs are new ones. Chromosomes are not new, but somehow, we are substantially different than our relative, the chimpanzee. It is as if Chimpanzee had mutated from a basic human to become what it is today. I know that is hard to believe, so I will fill in more holes. Our next stop is 55 hundreds years ago.

8 Major Mutations

Between 5 and 6 thousand years ago a huge blast of mutations hits our DNA and changed us forever. While 50% of the major mutations had occurred around the time of the Pleistocene Extinction, The remaining 50% of the major mutations occurred when there was no extinction recorded; or was there? The following is a short list of those changes from the ones we looked at from the Pleistocene Extinction.

- L-Dravidian India
- M- Western Asian
- P-Proto-European
- Q- Northern American
- R- Scythian [Balkan]
- R1- Aryan
- S-Melanesian
- T-Georgian
- ?-Chimpanzee
- ?-Bonobo
- ?-Vanara

For this book I am presenting the possibility that there were three additional DNA mutations not registered by Haplotype DNA scientists as the DNA was significantly altered for all three so we will have to rely on historical records for some of this. Before I get to that, let's see what happened to the genetic Engineers who had made dinosaurs during the Pleistocene. The knowledge must have between passed along as dinosaurs were recreated---a second time.

Holocene Dinosaurs

Many ancient texts talk about the manufacture of these animals, but right now let's look at a second <u>RE-MAKING of massive animals</u> to show just how good these genetic scientists really were. This time we are talking about after the great Pleistocene Extinction. Our first stop is Egypt and Sumeria.

Egyptian Dinosaurs

Everyone has seen the dinosaur from the tablet of Narmer, the first unifying King of Egypt. It is shown next left.

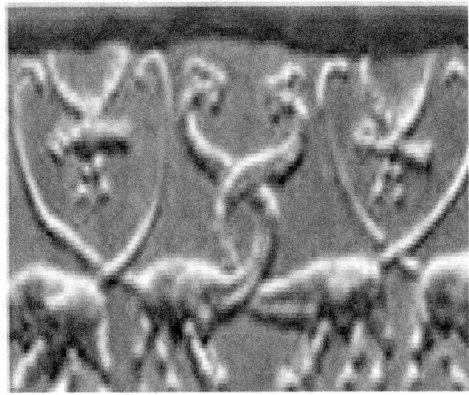

Sumerian Duplicate

Some may not know how very close Sumeria and Egypt was during the days after the Bharata War, but, the dinosaur images above right are from Sumeria and an almost identical match even to the crossing of the necks. To show how close these 2 groups were, let's quickly look at the tablet of the first Egyptian king after the Bharata War whose name was

Narmer or Naram. It is shown next left and contains the dinosaurs.

To the right is one of the first Kings of Sumeria after the war whose name was Naram. I'm not going into the similarities, but let me just give you one more odd similarity called the nose pull. While it is shown on the Egyptian Narmar's stone [below left], next to it is a similar one from Sumeria and no details of this unusual practice is registered in either country.

Sorry for the nose thing, but no one seems to know why Egypt and Sumeria were so close. Both of these kings ruled just after the Bharata War. By this time, regenerated animals of all types had been made. The next collage shows some of the animals that have been depicted around the world from after ;the horrible war.

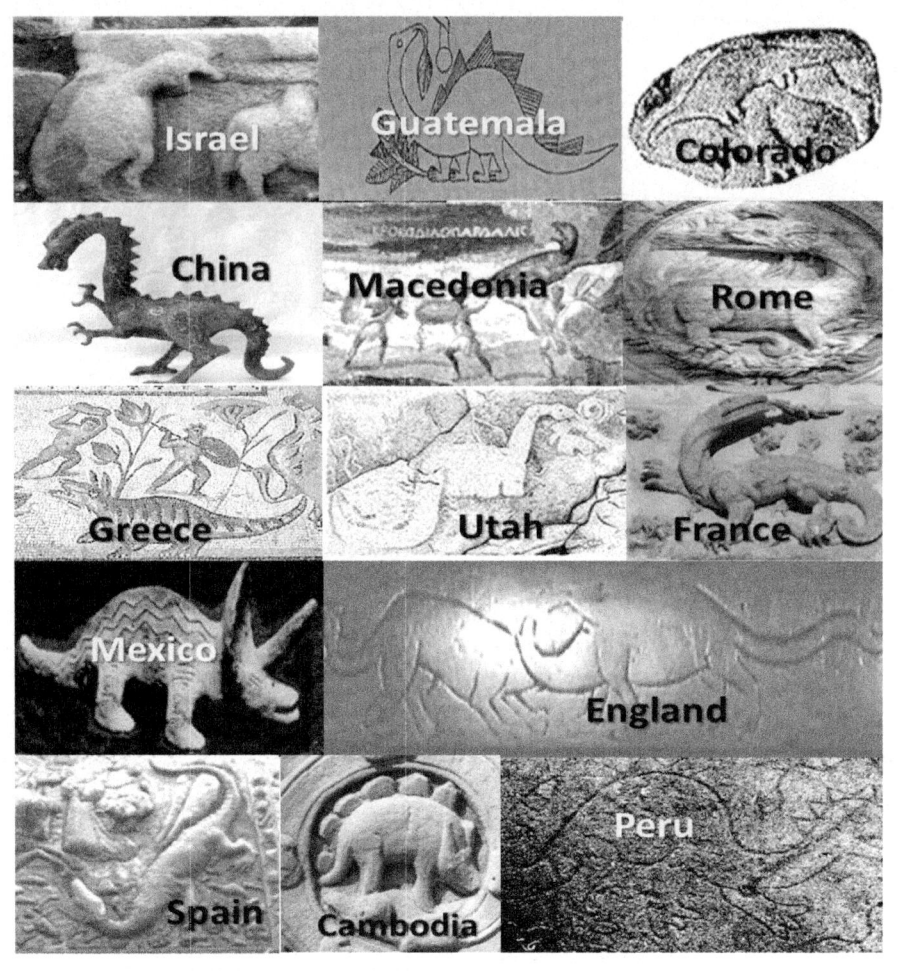

I know you can't see the tiny arms of the T-Rex in the image from Israel, but it is still believed they saw one or more of these regenerated monsters. Once you make all types of vicious and powerful animals including dragons and you manipulate the genetic codes by splicing in human DNA into others to make "half-human soldiers, the next thing to do would be to try to take over heaven. After all, these angels are certainly less than angelic. The reason I'm bringing up dragons is that I want you to see just how good the ancient scientists were at designing animals. Many of the animals were apes.

Tower of Babel War

I've been talking about the Bharata or Babel War for a while now, so I had better at least provide you with a little of the details. Ok! We had all kinds of experimenting and warring and ape making and finally there was a worldwide flood that killed almost everyone. A few of the scientists still survived and set up shop again. I know you are thinking that Noah carried all the animals, but then there would be no oddball kangaroo in Australia or all the other geo-specific animals we have around the world. Someone was making them all around even if you believe in evolution, the widely separated and distinct differences of animals at the various continents tells us that manipulation was occurring.

Tower of Babel

After a couple thousand years, people began to fight in a big way and a tower was built as some type of launching pad to initiate or continue a bloody war killing thousands of people. The genetic biologists got into the act and everything----I mean everything changed for mankind forever. It is my belief that they were experimenting with some germ to help win the war when it was let out in the atmosphere. It was a nasty little thing by all accounts. Another possibility was that use of nuclear weapons force many deaths and massive mutations. The ancient books of "Rig Veda", "Jasher", and others tell us what happened. The war was horrible and included nuclear weapons from the now famous and extremely ancient Oklo nuclear Processing plants that have enough nuclear material that has vanished to light up all of New York for a year. The Indian texts tell us that *animals would burst into flames* and *entire cities were destroyed by a single bomb*. The *fallout from the bombs would make everyone sick* and thousands died. The book of Jasher indicates that the wrath of God was brought out and *1/3 of the entire planet died, 1/3 were redeposited around the world* after having their brains "modified" they could no longer do some of the things they could do before the war. *They could not communicate without words*, for instance.

It is my contention that what caused the brain to suddenly not work properly was a germ that had been created. Somehow it affected the actual DNA and 90% of the brain became useless. Didn't you ever wonder why we only use 10% of our brains today? Didn't you wonder why the Neanderthal and Cro-Magnon brains were larger than ours is today. It is as if our brain was no longer being used and began to atrophy like the appendix. Didn't you wonder how idiot savants can tap into one of the sections that are useless and be able to play a piano flawlessly without ever learning how? This bioengineered germ messed up the entire World. The "Genesis" book simply talks about how we had to start talking verbally to communicate.

Genesis 11:1[before the war] Now the whole earth had one language and <u>few words</u>. [Notice it says that people used very few spoken words. The only way that could be possible is that most communication was done without words. After the germ was let out we had to relearn speaking.]

Oh! I already told you what happened to the remaining 1/3 of the population, according to Jasher. They became as monkeys.

Before we get into the monkey thing in more depth, let me provide some of the many texts detailing this fateful day in our history and in the history of apes.

Jasher 8:32-33- *And God said to the seventy angels who stood foremost before him, to those who were near to him, saying, Come let us descend and <u>confuse their tongues</u>, that one man shall not understand the language of his neighbor, and they did so unto them. And from that day following, they forgot each man his neighbor's tongue, and <u>they could not understand to speak in one tongue</u>.* [If you can no longer understand and if you forget you neighbor's tongue, something bad is happening to your intelligence level.]

Jasher 8:33-39- *And the Lord smote the three divisions that were there, and he punished them according to their works and designs. <u>Those who said, we will ascend to heaven and serve our gods, became like apes and elephants</u>.* [Nasty punishment] *Those who said, We will smite the heaven with arrows, the Lord killed them, one man through the hand of his neighbor; and those who were left amongst them, when they knew and understood the evil which was coming upon them, they forsook the building, and they also became scattered upon the face of the whole earth. --And many of the sons of men died in that tower, a people without number.* [Besides making people dumber in that they lost a level of communication capability there were three more punishments. Some were killed, some were transported to distant places, and the reset had something happen that made them similar to apes. If the brain capability is reduced, the people would have been apelike.]

Genesis 11:7-9- *Come, let us go down, and there confuse their language, that <u>they may not understand one another's speech</u>. -- Therefore its name was called Ba'bel, because there the LORD confused the language of all the earth.* [Notice something peculiar. As punishment for building a tower, people on the other side of the world and who were not involved in building the tower lost their language skills. This sounds like an indiscriminate germ.]

***Jubilees 10: 24-26**-And he confounded their language, and they no longer understood one another's speech, and they ceased then to build the city and the tower. For this reason the whole land of Shinar [mostly the country of Lebanon] is called Babel, because the Lord did there confound all the language of the children of men, and from thence they were dispersed into their cities, each <u>according to his language and his nation</u>.* [By saying it three times the writer is pretty sure, some limitation in man's capabilities occurred 5000 years ago and it happened to everyone on the earth, not just the tower builders.]

Try to Ignore the "turn into a monkey" Statement

While it would be easy to ignore the "turn into a monkey" portion of our ancient history, what we will find is that the monkey de-evolution concept was accepted worldwide as was the loss of brain power as our brains began to atrophy. Let's investigate some more.

South American Evidence

According to the "Popul Vuh" we find a similar story of the Atlantean "Babel" survivors. The Ancient Mayans indicated that the hybrids that had lived on the island named Aztalan had to leave suddenly. While this was an aggravation, it didn't seem to matter to them because they controlled their environment and just about everything else. By the text, this environmental control may have included places in Outer Space. All in all the PreBabel Aztalaneans were much smarter than post Babel variants.

They [the ancient ones], had the power of understanding;

They saw and could immediately see far [Possibly telescopes or really good eyes.]

They succeeded in knowing everything that could be seen or known in the world. Things that were hidden in the distance they could see without moving first. [Possibly reference some ability for out-of-body movement or a form of television]

Their wisdom was great; they controlled the forests, the rocks, the lakes, the seas and the valleys. [This was some kind of control over nature, although they were not able to save their island homeland.]

They investigated the four corners of the earth. [Traveled to faraway places]

They investigated the four corners of heaven. [experienced extended space travel]

They investigated the round surface of the earth. [Circumnavigated the globe]

After explaining the capabilities of the Aztalaneans, the texts then goes on to tell about what happened after the famous "Tower of Babel debacle".

Then one day the heart of heaven blew fog in their eyes, **[God confounded the people because of the Tower of Babel War.]**

They could not see clearly any more, like breathing on a mirror. **[God made them less intelligent]**

Their eyes were covered and they could only see things that were nearby. **[God limited their vision]**

This was the way that the wisdom and knowledge of these first people was destroyed. [In Jewish version of the Tower of Babel, some of the survivors were turned into apes. Just like the Jewish version the Atlantean survivors of the Tower of Babel War lost the ancient knowledge of the "first people".]

While the Jewish version of what happened is not as detailed in some ways, it is obvious that both texts are talking about the same instance and both are saying that 5 to 6 thousand years ago, man lost many capabilities that he once enjoyed. One of the capabilities was, as Genesis put it, "speaking without words". In fact, man lost many of his previous capabilities and became ignorant. While the entire human race had suffered massive mutations which affected our thinking ability, there were some who suffered worse defects.

While they don't talk about war, they do recognize the oddness of the mass mutation. Let's see what Geneticists tell us.

While for a long time there were not many mutations, the human genetic diversity today is vastly different from what 200 generations ago. A study dating the age of more than 1 million single-letter mutations in the human DNA code *reveals that <u>most of these mutations are of recent origin.</u> <u>Over **86 percent of the harmful single nucleotide mutations** arose **between 5 and 11 thousand years ago**</u>. Oddly, since then there have been few mutations at all. Overall, researchers now believe that <u>about 81 percent of the single-nucleotide variants in the European sampled and **58 percent in the African DNA sampled arose in the past 5,000 years**</u>.*

About half of the major mutation of the human race occurred 11 thousand years ago during the Pleistocene War and Extinction period and most of the rest of the major mutations occurred after the Bharata War.

Evidence-While there is tons of evidence of the use and destruction by nuclear materials during these volatile times, let me just point out a few.

- The 16 Ancient Nuclear Processing facilities located in Gabon, Africa is missing enough processed Uranium to power New York City for a year. ----or build bombs
- During the Young Dryas [11 thousand years ago, huge spike of radioactivity and other signs of nuclear events were recorded showing the Earth's atmosphere was saturated in some type of nuclear fallout..
- Many unfossilized Tyrannosaurs Rex bones not only show they lived 20 thousand years ago or so [a process of remanufacturing animals similar to that Jurassic Park movie] but also they are <u>so radioactive, they must be painted with lead</u> based paint to protect viewers.
- The City of Mohen jo Daro [mound of the dead] was left filled with the remains of bodies, melted walls and clay pots that had turned into balls of glass.
- Interestingly, in a sick way, the human remains scattered all over Mohen jo Daro <u>are still radioactive</u>.
- Around the world we are finding massive colonies of people who moved to underground cities 5 thousand years

ago to protect themselves for something on the surface. Many underground cities were found in Turkey, Malta, China, Scotland, Mexico, Peru, the U.S.A, and just about everywhere else.

Many ancient texts tell of the horrors of the war but I think the "Book of Jasher" gives a good indication of Mutations.

Jasher 7:19-20- the name of the first son of Eber was Peleg, for in his days all the sons of men were divided, and in the latter days, the entire earth was divided. [in War] And the name of the second son was Yoktan, meaning that in his day the lives of the sons of men were diminished and lessened. [In this mutation a normal lifespan in excess of a thousand years was changed to less than 200 years.]

Jasher 9:27-33 And when they were building they built themselves a great city and a very high and strong tower; and on account of its height the mortar and bricks did not reach the builders in their ascent to it, until those who went up had completed a full year, and after that, they reached to the builders and gave them the mortar and the bricks [The huge citadel and; thus was it done daily. -let us[God's angels] descend and confuse their tongues---And from that day following, they forgot each man his neighbor's tongue. the Lord confounded the Language of the whole earth; behold it was at the east of the land of Shinar and its circumference is three days' walk.. [This mutation limited the capabilities of the brain. Therefore it began to atrophy, making our brains shrink from its 1600cm^3 to our current 1300 cm^3 over the past 5000 years.]

Jasher 9:35 The 1/3 who said, We will ascend to heaven and serve our gods, became like apes and elephants. The 1/3 who said, we will smite the heaven, the Lord killed them, one man through the hand of his neighbor. The third division of men who said, we will ascend to heaven and fight, the Lord scattered them throughout the earth. [One third of the Earth remained in a livable state, 1/3 died in the wars, and a third of all the earth mutated into what we will call the Vanara people]

Called the Bharata War by in the Indian histories, this time of massive mutation of all the people of the world was a horrible time not brought out in many classrooms. Some of the mutations were noted by major changes in how long people lived or how they could use their massive brain, but the worst mutation was more than simply establishing a new race of people called the Vanara.

Vanara People

OK! Ape lovers and those who act like apes, here is your section of our history that really amplifies the ape. It is kind of like reverse evolution. While the book of Jasher also indicated that some were turned into elephants, it is the apes we are talking about in this book so that is where we are heading. You have to admit that turning people into something similar to an ape was certainly a most interesting punishment that God could have accomplished and it would be easy. As we have been examining, our DNA is almost identical to an Ape and with a simple twist or pull on a DNA string and we would be climbing trees right now. I know I'm sounding silly here and I don't mean to. This is serious and it was a horrible time for many. Around the world people actually became apelike and there is proof. What we find is that, all of a sudden, people from around the world began to recognize apes as human or even heroes and it all started exactly during the time the Tower was falling down. The affected people may have lost almost all knowledge of civilization and had to start over. Besides the reverence, many of the flood stories that were written down also talked about the horrible change and how people became monkeys or apes. The people that recorded this event include the people of the Congo, the Totonacs, the Aztecs, and several others. All of these people indicated that some of the people became monkey-like some time after the flood. If something took away preflood knowledge and took away telepathic speech from everyone, or a virulent germ attacked our DNA, just a slight increase in the ignorance blast could have reduced the knowledge and characteristics of many a little more. It is not so unreasonable, given the possibility of eliminating telepathy nor does it go against any evidence that has been found to date. Whenever many groups of people say the same thing, the probability that it is the truth becomes more likely. Let's read the histories so we can test probability.

Essene Evidence-*Jasher 8:33-39- Those who said, we will ascend to heaven [1/3 of the people] and serve our gods, became like apes.*

Totonac- Mexican Tradition-*After the flood, the boat finally rested and God reversed man's face and hind parts and turned him into a monkey.* [Probable indication of man turning to monkeys after the Babel incident]

Mayan Tradition-*During the second creation, people turned into monkeys and the world was destroyed by wind.* [Possibly talking about the destruction of Babel and another indication of people turning into monkeys]

Aztec History-*During the age of the four winds men turned into monkeys according to Codex "Laticano-Vatino"* [Possibly wind destroyed the tower and the monkey thing keeps coming back.]

The Lower Congo Tradition-*"First God created man. After a huge flood, men put their milk stick behind them and were turned into monkeys."* [Some men became primitive after the flood as was indicated after the Babel incident]

Tibetan History-*"Tibet was almost totally inundated by the flood. The survivors had been little better than monkeys. The god Gya sent teachers to civilize the people and they repopulated the land after the flood."*

Indian History

India has a rich history filled with ape-men during the time of the Bharata War. Their 2 main religious historical works, Ramayana and Mahabharata are filled with the descriptions and events associated with the devolved people known as the Vanara.

Ramayana I 17:8-18*- Vanaras [ape-people] are created by Brahma to help Rama in battle against Ravana. They are powerful and have many godly traits. Taking Brahma's orders, the gods began to parent sons in the semblance of monkeys. They are powerful and have many godly traits.* It presents them as humans with reference to their speech, clothing, habitations, funerals, consecrations and describes their monkey-like characteristics such as their leaping, hair, fur and a tail. Some were turned in anger. *One of the gods*[Anak] *Gautama, had a daughter named Anjana. Anjana told her father about Indra visiting his wife while he was away. So his wife cursed her daughter to turn into a monkey. Gautama cursed his two boys to turn into monkeys as well as they had failed to inform him of the same. He could not retract the curse and so he gave all three monkeys to Riksha, the monkey-king of Kishkindha. anaras are created by Brahma to help Rama in battle against Ravana. ----After Vanaras were created they began to organize into armies and spread across the forests, although some, including Hanuman, stayed with ":Normal" humans. The evil king of Sri Lanka, Ravana, kidnapped Prince Rama's wife Sita. He and the Vanara army led by Hanuman battle against Ravana. Two of the Vanara, Nala and Nila, built a bridge over the ocean so that Rama and the army could cross to Sri Lanka, kill Ravana, save Sita, and bring peace to all of India.*

Mahabharata - Like Ramayana, this set of sacred Hindu books describes the Vanara ape-people as forest dwellers, and mentions 2 of their kings doing battle with and being defeated by a Pandava general who led a military campaign to south India. It also makes a big deal about Hanuman as being from the gods [Anak people] of that time. To save Princess Sita, Hanuman leaped the distance between India and Sri Lanka to save her. Another story has Hanuman going through a tunnel system to a new world.

What is the Real Story?

We are actually going to talk about 3 different types of ape-like mutations of man from this horrible war. Hopefully you are beginning to believe that there might have been truth in the many different and generally isolated writings. I know it still sounds absurd to you, but just about every society is telling us that it did happen and there is much more evidence to come. If we assume for a minute that hundreds of ancient people were not completely wrong in their observations, it would be interesting to trace the histories of these unfortunate people. Some horrible mutations did not kill but instead converted people back to looking ape-like. The Ramayana from India called these people the Vanara so let's use that name for the horrible disfigured mutation that was sensed almost over the world. All we can assume at this time is that a large group of humans had mutated by chemical, biological, or nuclear fallout means. Possibly they devolved back to Homo-Erectus people or something similar, but these unfortunate people became useful in the societies of that time and many were well respected. From the information in the book of Jasher, we can believe as many as 1/3 of the population of the world was mutated in this or a similar way. Like many mutations like donkey and burro, they cannot procreate and would have died off if it weren't for the back breeding with horses. Soon we find no more about the once great ape-men from the Bharata War Era, but the certainly not before they made a huge impression on the people of that time..

Vanara, Egypt and Electricity

Around the world we find that ape-people had been integrated into society. We can believe in a family might have been born several normal children and one that was ape-like. If it were not so, this group would have certainly been shunned. We find the opposite. We find an integrated Vanara/Ape-Race.

What do Ape-people, Egypt, and Electricity have in common? The answer or at least the question is found on pictures in a temple in Dendera as shown below. These pictures depict something people like to call the Dendera tube. Two of these devices are shown below left. The devices appear to be electronic and ape-men are depicted with them as shown on the depiction to the right.

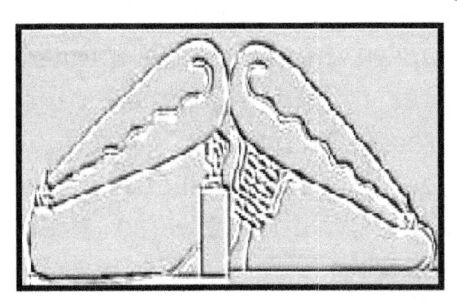

If that were the only depiction, no one would think too much about it, but more and more were found. The following group of pictures below depicts some type of electronic tube-like objects resting on still other strange devices. These things seem to be all held up by a little human who tries to point the main device at an ape-man. While we are talking about people becoming ape-like, the ape character was also the sign of the magician, Thoth. We can believe the ape-people we generally just as intelligent as the other people, but their DNA had been mangled be "something". Let me show you some examples. You can clearly see the Ape-man on drawings below. The ape-men seem to be different than the Thoth image, so one may expect that they represent those unfortunates that were turned into apes as punishment for the Babel War. I know it's a crazy notion, but there are plenty more images that don't have more acceptable explanations.

Dendera Tube and Electricity

As I mentioned, the big tubes being held on these depictions are called Dendera tubes. I've got to tell you that these "Dendera tubes", by their very looks, must have used some kind of electricity. The twisted cabling to their base, the filament like internal structure, and the radiation type insulator holding the one on the right below all point to the same conclusion. While I'm not getting into a discussion about how the Great Pyramid of Giza was used to manufacture electricity during our past, let's just assume that it did or something else generated electricity in the olden days. This Dendera tube thing could have been one of the devices that used the valuable resource. Cables are attached to the "Dendera tubes".

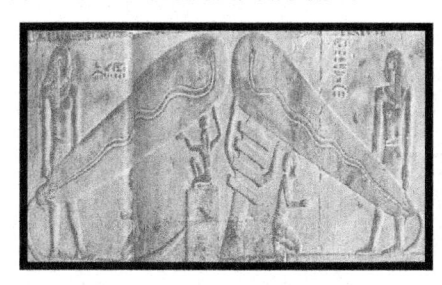

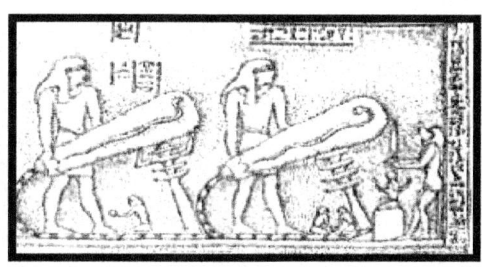

The electricity would have been used to make these things radiate in some way. The radiating component was somehow important so we should recognize that the tubes produced something special. There is something else you should recognize. There is a <u>miniaturized image of Pharaoh</u> under the left Dendera tube on all the carvings. This indicates that the pharaoh needed whatever this machine produced and the pharaoh was insignificant with respect to the Dendera Tube. These things must have been really something to be more important that a pharaoh.

The first and third images show a huge ape-man guard wielding a knife, evidently to protect the Dendera tubes, so here is my theory, for what it's worth.

Maybe the thing had something to do with keeping the demigod rulers [like pharaoh] alive after the tree of life was lost in the worldwide flood. The Ape-men were hired to make sure most people did not live as long as the rulers.

Some show streams of energy emanating and the Vanara are standing by or holding a scarab above it.

From the end of the tube, it simply looks like a shining orb. Many of the depictions are shown this was and the faithful Vanara people seem to be worshiping the orb along with regular humans.

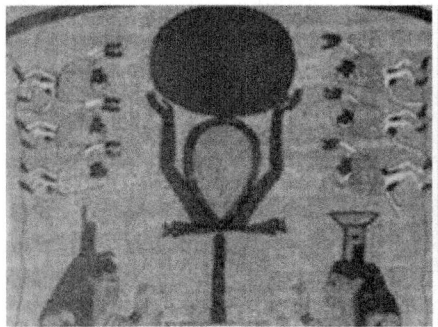

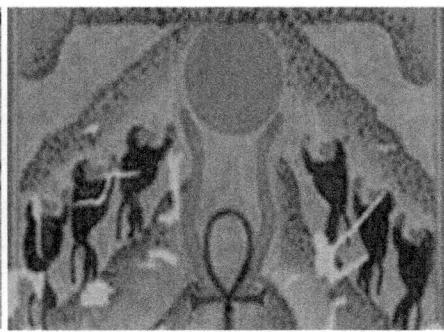

178

Sometimes the "orb" was sitting on top of a bird and still the Vanara worshipped and protected it as shown in the next set of images.

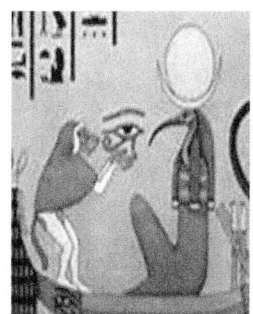

Whatever these energy devices were, they started show up everywhere. Here is the obvious statement. If you hired ape-men to guard this most valuable thing, they must have been quasi-human apes around at the time. We will see that these ape-men were well established in the Egyptian culture of this time even besides being honored guards for whatever the Dendera tubes were used for. Right now, let me show you that these tubes were not just in Egypt.

More Energy Radiators

Sumerian Radiators-These Dendera tubes were found all over the place and I suppose there were Apes that could be hired to guard them all over as well. Read the section below from the "Epic of Gilgamesh" and see if this could have been describing the Dendera Tube energy.

Sumerian Epic of Gilgamesh- *Upon the corpse, hung from the pole, they* ***directed the pulse and the radiance****; 60 times the water of life, 60 times the food of life, they sprinkled upon it; and Inanna arose* [Sounds like some kind of electric shock treatment, used to bring Inanna back to life. Could the pictured apparatus have been the device used to deliver the directed pulse??]

Picture of the Device-We may have a picture of the ancient Sumerian form of the Dendera tube. On the seal above left can be seen a tube with some kind of rays emanating away from it. The device looks very much like the Dendera Tubes. We can call this one the "Sumerian Tube" if you like. The only difference is that fish men have replaced the baboon and one of those Merkaba flying machines found everywhere is flying overhead. Let me just say right now, I don't believe people turned into fish. You can see they are only wearing fish costumes

Really good Dendera tubes might even have flying ships with multiple people riding as the Sumerian seal preceding right implies. Only one fish guy is shown here, but the depictions are always the same. This does not mean ape-men were not in Sumeria.

Assyrian Radiating Tubes-Here are some examples of the Assyrian version of the Dendera Tube. In this depiction, the radiator seems to have "fruit" making it more probable that the ancient Anak people made artificial "Tree-of-Life fruit with the device. A Merkaba [Flying Machine] is still dancing overhead just like in the Sumerian version [No one is wearing fish costumes].

To the right is another image from Assyria. The men have changed clothes again, but the rest is the same. The Assyrian artifact flowers and eagle-headed people pick the fruit. This could have been showing that the Dendera tube was making fruit like an artificial Tree-of-Life or some type of important "fruit".

Central American Radiators-The Aztecs and Mayans both depicted "radiating tubes" of some kind. Something shoots out of the Aztec version while the Mayan one shows an internal filament similar to the Dendera tubes of Egypt.

The Aztecs must also have known about this device as well. The Codex Nuttal [Below left] shows the device. Some kind of radiating beam is coming from the central orb. The device is standing by what appears to be a rocket and a throne. While there are no ape-men in this drawing an ape was one of the Aztec god images.

Guatemala-The Mayans also depicted a radiating tube of some kind as shown in this page of the Dresden Codex [See above middle-upper central image]. Notice that the filament

181

of the device has the same forked look like the Egyptian model. I drew it larger for clarity of the filament design.

. Indian Radiator

In India a similar radiating tube was depicted, but this one seems to be somewhat different in that a person gets inside the tube. It certainly was no simple light bulb. [See next left]. Compare it to the ones from Assyria and Sumaria. Possibly if those people wearing fish costumes had gotten inside they would have lived longer.

Who Protected Dendera Tubes?

Let me talk in a little more depth about something that is very curious and related to this whole evolution and modification of Homo Sapiens and Erectus and these "ape-people" who were so trusted that they would guard the most precious items. Humans mostly mutated into races just before the end of the Pleistocene and a second time around 5500 years ago during what was called the Bharata War during which the book of "Jasher" tells us 1/3 of the population of the entire world lost their lives and another third became like Apes. The Indian ancient histories called them the Vanara. They spoke, wore normal clothing, worked with "normal" people, and battled the evil that continued to plague India after Vanaras organized into armies. After some time they died off as if their Procreation was almost impossible. In Cambodia many ape-men statues protect the Ankor-Watt temple. In ancient Mexico, one their sacred gods was depicted as an ape-man. On and on we could go, but soon the Ape-men were gone as the mutation must not have been sustainable in procreation. Ape-men didn't simply protect Dendera Tubes; some or many were important people of the community and even revered as heroes. The Egyptians believed in an Ape god. While we are on the subject of an Ape-man being considered the magician-god named Thoth, we also need to go around the world including Mexico and Cambodia and investigate a similar strangeness. Many places worshipped these hairy humanoids, which may or may not help us understand what happened to some of the people after the Tower of Babel incident. At least it will show how revered the ape-man was. We might not completely understand what the ancient historians meant by telling us about the transformation from human to ape-like human, but one thing is certain; around the world there were apes that were very human. They came on the scene around 6 thousand years ago and were completely gone from the earth by 3 thousand years ago. Let's see what else the post-Babelic ape-men/Vanara were up to.

More Ape-Men Heroes

Egypt Ape-men were depicted as worshiping some type of orb at a <u>higher level than the "normal" humans</u>. They were certainly not depicted as animals. Could some of the punished humans have been in Egypt? [The orb could be another representations of one of those Dendera tubes as shown next left. They were certainly not depicted as animals. Could some of the punished humans have been in Egypt?

Bird Headed Ape-men-Sometimes the Egyptian ape-like people wore bird heads, but they still could defeat humans and evidently did by this depiction as dead or dying "regular people lay under their feet.

By the way, just about everywhere you turn in Egypt you find depitions of one of these Vanara Ape-men. They were revered, and used in many setting as guards, and protectors of religious artifacts.

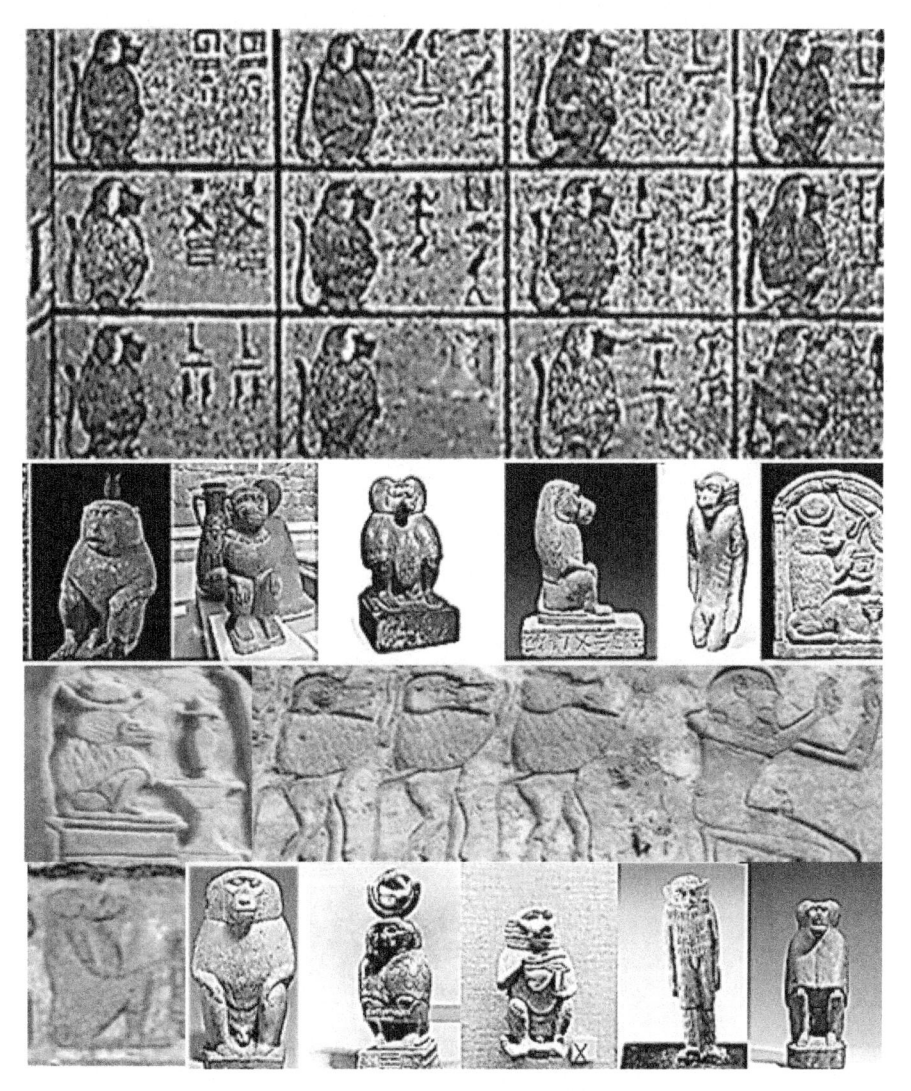

We find the same depictions in the Far East.

Far Eastern Apes Men

*Cambodia-*The ancient capital city of Cambodia is called Ankor-Watt. Similar ape-men appear to be guarding the entrances to the temples—who knows? [first 2 rows in next collage.

Bali- We find the same thing in other parts of Indonesia and SE Asia as the images show in the following collage. While there certainly are regular monkeys and apes in this region, the sheer number and descriptions depicted showing almost human facial expression and features assure us that these unfortunate people were members of society during this post Bharata time.

***India*-I** As I mentioned earlier, in Indian history, the Vanara play heavily in Indian history. Here are a few of the hundreds of images, statues, paintings etc.

Ape-men soldiers fought along the side of their hero Rama, who was battling his brother, an evil "god/Anak". Below are still more images. From the looks of their wounds, they were

187

in trouble. The one with 12 holes is Rama. [See above right] In Sri Lanka, the Hindu ape-god named Hanuman escaped the flames of a burning city. [See the following images].

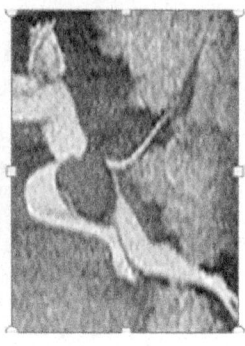

African Nomoli- There is no telling how many places the Vanara lived in around the world but we can believe ape-men who had been part of the Western African society lived during the time of the Vanara. This time they would be called the Nomoli. Today there is not much in Sierra Leon, but there are diamonds so many search. Instead of diamonds they kept finding these Nomoli statues. No one knew why they were on the ground characterized as partially apes, they mostly squatted, had huge round ears and the muzzle of an ape, but they were also human-like very similar to the Vanara described in India. One legend in the area says: *The part of the sky in which the Nomoli lived turned to stone. It splintered and fell to Earth as pieces of rock.* Anopther legend indicated that *angels had once lived in the Heavens. One day, as a punishment for causing bad behavior, God turned the angels into humans and sent them to Earth. The Nomoli figures serve as representations of those figures, and as a reminder of how they were banished from the Heavens and sent to Earth to live as humans.* Another legend indicated that *the statues represent the former kings and chiefs of the Sierra Leone region.* There were indications that an ancient group called the Temne would perform ceremonies during which they would <u>treat the figures as if they were the ancient leaders</u>. The following collage is a small sampling of the huge number of these figurines reminding us that some became like apes as the book of Jasher told us.

We even know the statues were made around the end of the Bharata War, before the eventual loss of DNA messaging which caused memory and capability loss. When one of the Nomoli statues was cut open, a small, perfectly spherical metal ball made our of steel and chromium fell out which we only now are able to process. The image following shows the ball that was exposed after a hole was made and the x-ray of the statuette is shown in the middle.

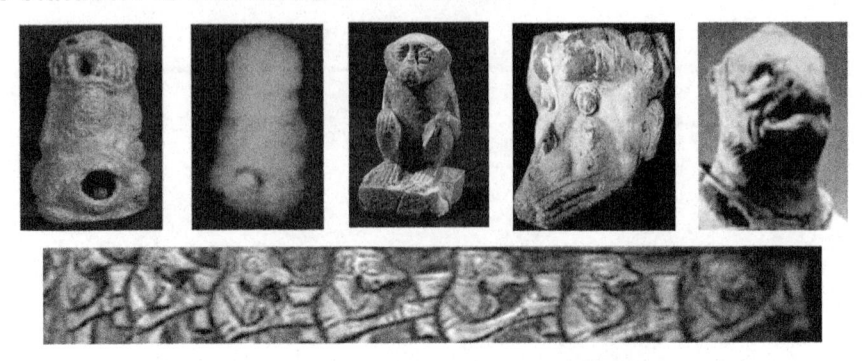

Eurasia- While we can probably find evidence of Nomoli or Vanara all over, the image above middle was found in Israel, the next from Asia, and the last from Japan. Below that is a procession of them from Sumeria and we find similar image in the Americas.

Central American Vanara

Honduras -legend says that local people worshipped huge '*Monkey Sculptures*'. American adventurer Theodore Morde claimed that sacrifices were made by local Indians to a gigantic idol of an ape. [pSee images to the left below.

Mexico-The Aztecs have Quetzalcoatl. Like the Egyptian ape-gods, he was a baboon and a human. There is a fairly high probability that Thoth and Quetzalcoatl were the same mutated human. Below middle is a picture of the Aztec version.

Panama-Mayans were no different than the Aztecs. They also worshipped apes. This effigy is in the form of a footstool or platform. [See preceding top 2nd from right]

Maya of Ecuador-In Ecuador, this monkey god was revered. [See preceding top right] Why would the ancient people of Ecuador revere this backward looking half human unless some of the leaders were monkey-like? The ape-man death god of the Maya is shown second row right]

South American Vanara

The possible discovery of *5000 years old Havan Kund* in Peru is believed by some to be the location Hanuman traveled to after a massive underground venture. The timing fits, but it is mostly here for completeness. The following image left shows the ancient site followed by ape-men effigies found in South America.

Where Are the Ape-men Now?

Possibly there were laws against intermarriage, but generally speaking the ape-people had jobs and held positions of authority. As the change was a DNA change, we can believe their offspring would have either amplified the characteristics or made the DNA structures more unstable. We know that chimpanzees, for instance have twice as many mutations in their DNA as humans attesting to the fact that their DNA is more unstable. With such a major change in DNA, we can believe marriages between normal and ape-people would not have successful offspring and the mutation rates of their offspring would have been amplified as the DNA bonding might have been more unstable than sequencing grounded by ancient development.

Hopefully, you are getting a stronger belief that there might have been truth in the many different and generally isolated writings. I know it still sounds absurd to you, but just about every society is telling us that it did happen and there is more evidence to come. If we assume for a minute that hundreds of ancient people were not completely wrong in their observations, it would be interesting to trace the histories of these unfortunate people. All we can assume at this time is that a large group of humans had some of their "human" genes removed leaving more of the hairy ape-man characteristics like Homo-Erectus man. The offspring of these "punished" individuals possibly became more hairy, and even had a more ape-like appearance just like the Homo Erectus had previously.

The ancient references do not indicate if these humans were transported to another location as was done with the other 1/3 of the population, so we can possibly assume that many stayed in a Middle Eastern location. This group must have quickly inbred others with similar characteristics and regained a place in our society. We can assume they had limited procreative capability and continuation of their species must have been a very hard road. Finally the instability of their DNA finally would not allow for breeding and they were finally lost to history. Whatever happened, the inbreeding has now completely removed this "special group of APE-humans", but at one time there may have been "apelike" humans and that time wasn't millions of years ago. Possibly there still are throwbacks.

Modern Monkey Tails

While tails are generally a sign of a monkey rather than an ape, for the purposes of this book all primates outside homo-sapiens are put into the same category. In India, the monkey tail is back. The first image below is a boy with an actual tail revered by the Hindu zealots as some type of their incarnate hero. The Ape god Hanuman has returned! The boy just thinks it's something to sit on as the ape tail is beginning to reappear. The question might be, "Are some monkey or ape characteristics returning?"

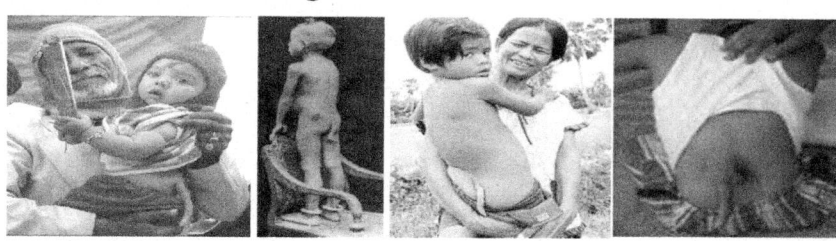

We are seeing more and more monkey tails reemerging as well as other scary features. While we all start off with a monkey tail as shown below, many times the tail is lost in the development process.

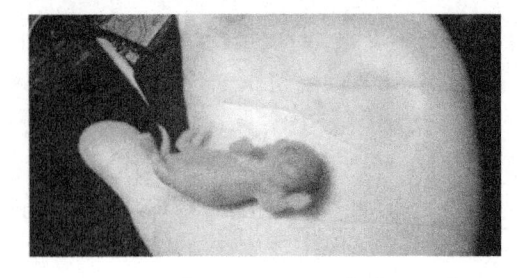

Unfortunately more and more people are retaining the tail possibly as DNA combinations are just matching up or there may be some mutation bringing us closer to apes again. Here are a few more examples.

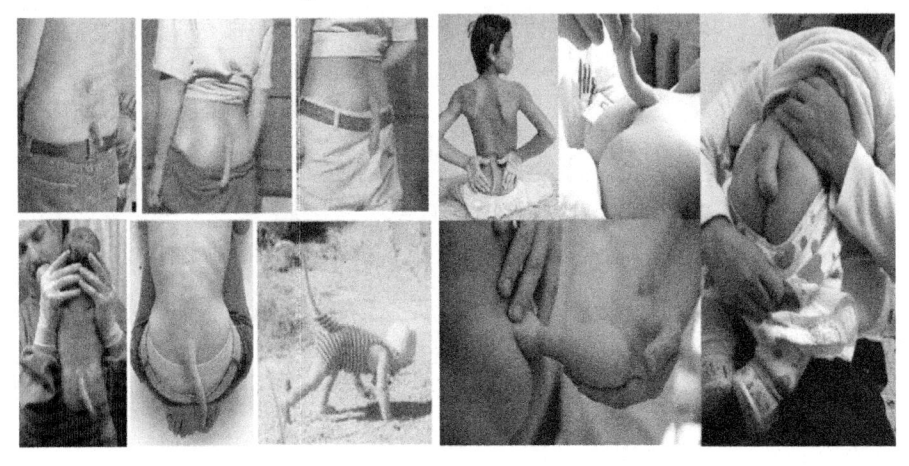

Year after year the quantity of people with this new characteristic seems to be increasing which suggests a reemergence of the features of the post Babel Ape-men, Who knows. Besides the disfiguring mutations I've been addressing, there were more serious ones that were done either intentionally or from nuclear fallout, or from some biologic agent, but we can be pretty sure, two other massive mutations occurred besides the Vanara devastation. Those were the Chimpanzee and Bonobo Mutations. Unlike the Vanara, The last two mutations were even more severe but they allowed for procreation so these devolved humans are still around.

Devolved Humans

To discuss this horrible DNA event we must include both the Bonobo and Chimpanzee. Chimpanzee and Bonobo DNA are very similar to humans. Some estimate the similarity to be 98%. That is a slight misnomer, but for our purposes here, it is a good estimate. The main difference in all apes and humans is that the 2nd set of chromosomes has been split apart as shown again in the DNA sequences following. This makes the Chimpanzee and other apes have more chromosomes than a man, but characteristics are still very similar. While all the ape variants may have just been manipulated by the Pleistocene humans, we must also question why the Chimpanzee and Bonobo DNA shows such a short time for mutations and what happened to massive numbers of ape-people that were written about and described around the world. The normal chart is shown below as some common ancestor well after gorilla split from the homo-Sapien line. Some have pushed the separation back 50 thousand years, but there is more evidence indicating the split was only 5 or 6 thousand years ago around the time of the Bharata War.

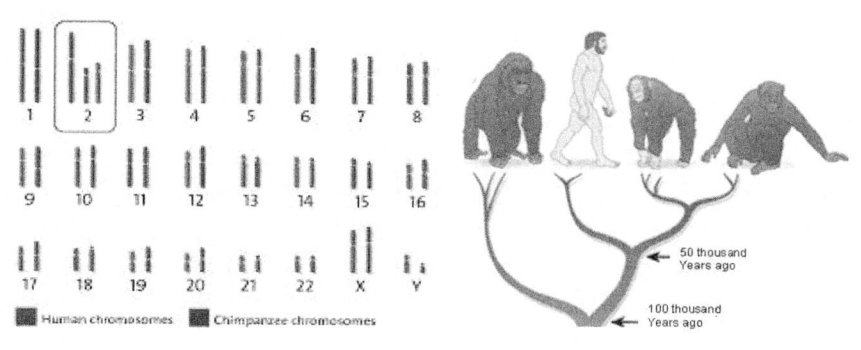

Today biologists are coming around and accepting the possibility of this very recent mutation from their own studies, but many have not connected the Bharata War with the emergence of these 2 primates.

Apes After the War

This may seem odd to you but let's investigate anyway. This whole Chimpanzee thing seems like the Gorilla would be the close relative, but it was not. The reason Chimpanzee can use tools so very well is that his closest relative, man, can use them. One possibility is that the brain reducing, DNA changing germ, or whatever it was made some die, some just lost brain capacity some became like apes and a small quantity became chimpanzee. The world had been at war and nuclear weapons had flattened much of the landscape. The Great Tower and citadel of Babel [Baalbek] had been flattened. All of a sudden, chimpanzees appeared. While we're on the subject of chromosomes, the similarities between chimpanzee and human genes, what is important is that, scientists <u>tell us our brain function chromosome patterns are 80% different than those of the chimpanzee</u>. It seems that as the body changes, other characteristics had to change with them. Possibly if we could see a live Homo-Erectus human, we would see a much closer resemblance.

Evolution suggests that only our heads were allowed to evolve while our bodies were stuck in an unevolved state.

As I mentioned before there are twice as many "small" mutations of Chimpanzee DNA over a given time than humans. This suggests the unstable nature of Chimpanzees and possibly other apes as they may all have been manufactured from humans at one time or another.

I'm not spending a lot of time on this subject but it, unfortunately, does tie in to Homo Erectus as the chimpanzee structure seems to be similar to the first Homo-Erectus or even earlier ape-men. The idea that ancient humans used and abused nuclear energy is distasteful to many so no one seems to want to talk about 2 of the worst wars we have ever had on our planet. The first happened about 11 thousand years ago causing about 50% of all major mutations on humans and the second one 5500 years ago caused the other 50%.

I know this is not what you learned in school as you were told Chimpanzee and Bonobo evolved separately from man as both separated from the Gorilla lineage about 4 million years ago. Today we know differently. One thing is for sure, while the evidence keeps mounting that ape-men were useful members of society between 3000 and 2000 BC. Evolutionist scientists backed by consensus rather than fact will continue to lie, disregard, and weave complex reasons for ignoring evidence to hold onto their sacred religion over the ancient Judeo-Christian religious details presented. Besides many documented elements supporting the Vanara and the images, and the statues, and the many leaps of faith required to believe what you were told in school. While we can expect at least one of the Vanara mutations would have been successful in procreation, many scientist don't even want to think about it. Let's test some of the things we are finding out about Chimpanzee and his cousin the Bonobo to see if it makes sense chimps came from man and, most likely as part of the mass mutation that occurred 5500 years ago.

Test number One

A few years ago, one group of researchers studied the genomes of 12 species of Drosophila or fruit fly, four species of nematode worm, and 10 species of primate, including humans. By comparing with other groups of species, they were able to estimate how long ago the genes were likely to have been acquired. Rather than by evolution, they determined that a number of genes, including the ABO blood group gene, were confirmed as having been acquired by vertebrates through intrusion of viruses, protists, fungi, and Bacteria. They confirmed 145 genes were acquired by this means to shape humans. <u>They found that 50 additional genes were "donated" in chimpanzee.</u>

Test number Two

DNA structure of Chimpanzee is almost a complete match with humans. While one of the chromosome strings has been split in Chimpanzee, the makeup of the DNA sugar is very close. The following image is of a Human, mouse, and chimp X chromosome containing about 1,100 different genes, or sets of instructions. Each gene affects a particular trait in the body. Each specific nucleotide that makes up a DNA string [adenine (A), thymine (T), guanine (G) and cytosine (C)] show up as a slightly different shade in the image below. Notice that the Chimpanzee and Human are virtually identical. This is very strange. You can see how different even the mouse DNA is. Even the Centromere [necked down area] is the same in chimps and men.

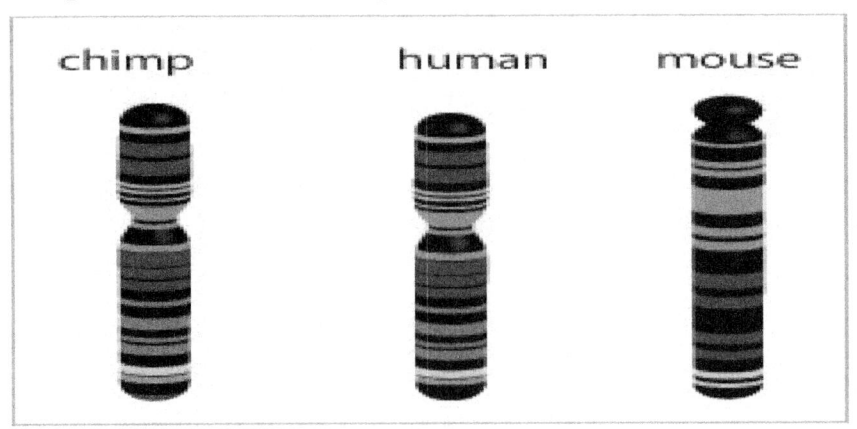

As I showed before just looking at DNA sequences of Orangutan, Gorilla, Chimpanzee and Modern human shows chimps and humans are especially close as most to the proteins line up exactly in line.

Test number Three

Human and chimp DNA was determined to be 1.2 percent different. Gorilla and other apes have over twice [3.1%] that much difference as they are somehow very different. In should be noted the genetic difference between individual humans today is minuscule – about 0.1%, on average. Now for the really weird part; bonobo has about 1.2% differences like chimps but Bonobo and Chimps have 1.6% difference between their DNA and Gorilla and other Apes.

Chimps and Bonobo are more closely related to humans than apes or even each other.

Test Number Four

At the end of each chromosome is a string of repeating DNA sequences called a telomere. Chimpanzees have about 23,000 base pairs of DNA that are repeated. While humans only have 10,000 base pairs of DNA repeats. One could determine that Chimps have not gone through as many mutations collecting these duplicates and is a newer species.

Test Number Five

It was determined that Bonobo was a mutated branch from Chimpanzee that occurred about a million years after the Chimpanzee and Human split 4 million years ago [using nuclear decay timing]. This has been augmented recently. In three separate studies it was determined that the human chimp split could have been only <u>6500 years ago</u> making the Bonobo split only about <u>5 thousand years ago</u>. [In 2001"*Phylogenetic And Familial Estimates Of Mitochondrial Substitution Rates: Study Of Control Region Mutation In Deep-Rooting Pedigrees*"; 1997. "*A High Observed Substitution Rate In The Human Mitochondrial DNA Control*

Region". In 2000. "The Mutation Rate In The Human MtDNA Control Region."]

Test Number Six

The following chart comes from the journal *"Nature"* and has nothing to do with me or the seemingly crazy details I am trying to tell you about. The reason I put it here is I wanted you to look at where they placed the "appearance" of chimpanzee up in the right hand corner around the same time as modern man. While they wanted to show commonly discussed species they did not try to determine hypothesized lines of descent, just when we believe they "appeared". Disregard the times as I discussed previously as this is using nuclear decay timing still.

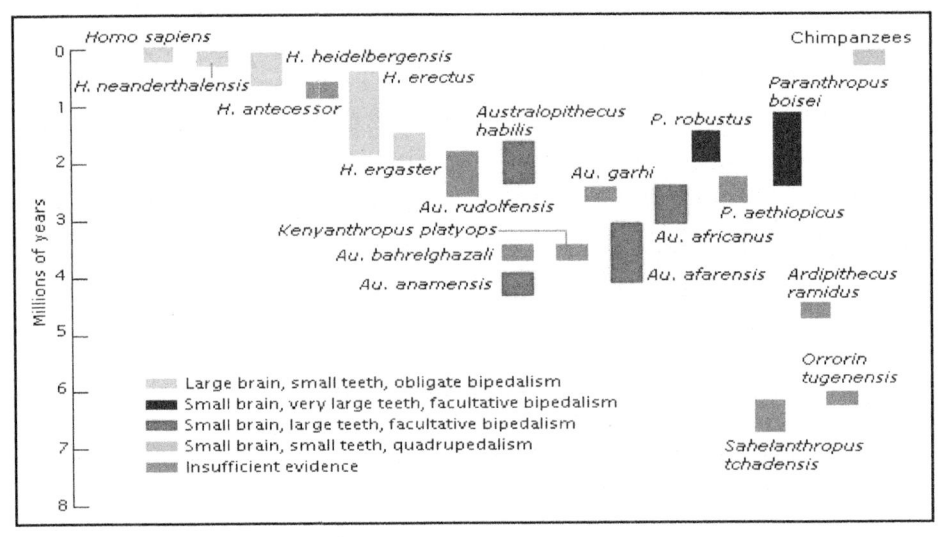

Test Number Seven

In the study, *"Bonobo Genome Compared With The Chimpanzee And Human Genomes"* Dr. Eichler and his colleagues found that the human and chimp sequences differ by only 1.2 percent in terms of single-nucleotide changes to the genetic code, but 2.7 percent of the genetic difference between humans and chimps are duplications, so we could really say it's only 1.1% difference. They also found that more than <u>3% of the human genome is more closely related to either the bonobo or the chimpanzee genome than these are to each other</u>. They also found almost a thousand integrations of transposons [Transposed similar sequences] absent from the orangutan but present in bonobo, chimpanzee, and human. Of these, 27 are shared between the bonobo and human genomes but are absent from the chimpanzee genome, and 30 are shared between the chimpanzee and human genomes but are absent from the bonobo genome. The images below are of the Bonobo, Homo-Erectus, and Chimpanzee, showing what the small changes do to a person. In addition, about 25% of human genes contain "parts" that are more closely related to one of the two apes than the other. This suggests that Bonobo did not necessarily split from Chimpanzee. It could have been a new mutation of Human.

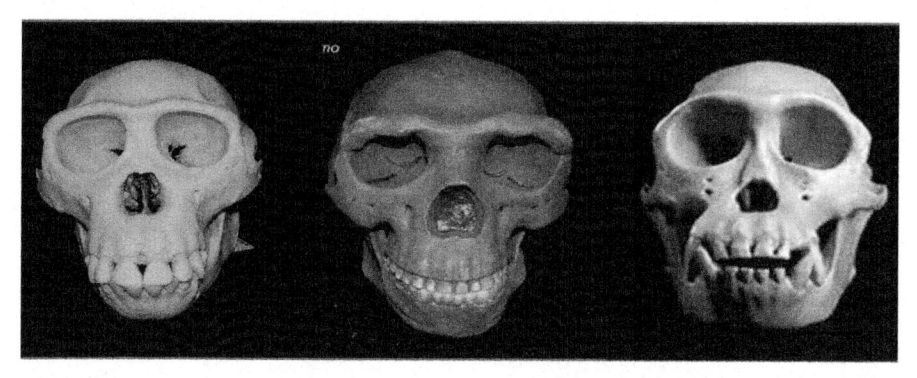

The following image compares Australopithicus, Erectus, Modern man, Bonobo and Chimpanzee skeletons. While the hips and hands have reverted back to Austropithicine style, there is a lot of similarity to the bonobo and chimp to homo-erectus. The bonobo is especially similar as noted from the skull and teeth similarity shown previously.

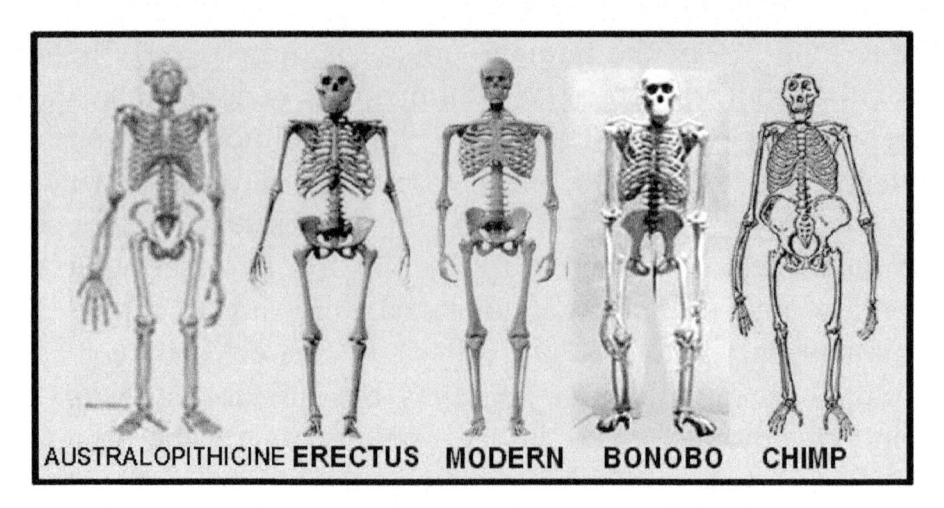

AUSTRALOPITHICINE **ERECTUS** MODERN BONOBO CHIMP

As the skeletons show Bonobo [left] probably have a closer relationship to humans than chimpanzee. The following images show bonobo mates are more similar in size which is a human trait, the hip is much smaller like humans, his profile shows a more similar structure, and his teeth are human.

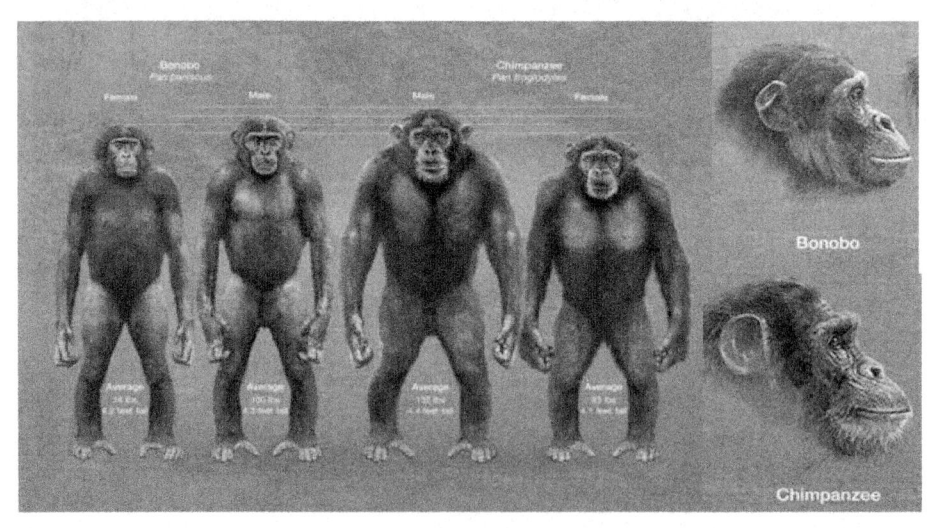

Sometimes Chimps are born with minimal hair as shown below. From these images we can better appreciate that chimps evolved from man. Yes their Arms are longer and legs are shorter and the pelvis is longer and wider, but chimpanzee seems to be a viable contribution to the idea of evolution as it looks like they evolved from us.

I'm not going to get into the horrors of this nuclear war in this book, but it seems we almost mutated ourselves back to Homo-Erectus by our stupidity 5 thousand years ago. The following description of the ape populations shows the strange bump in the road that produced chimpanzee. I corrected the timing according to the newer methodology as I would suspect some are not being taught this in our classrooms.

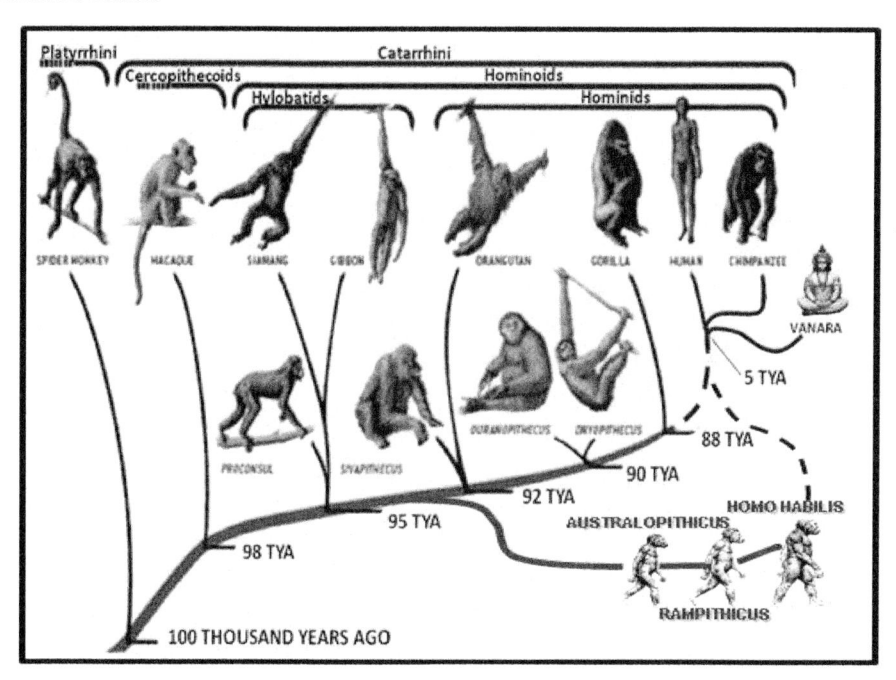

That brings us to cross breeding and DNA splicing, which is a much more serious issue.

Cross Breeding

Just like was done in the Tertiary and Pleistocene ages, we are now regenerating DNA modified animals at an alarming rate. As a clue, we are now seeing piglets with human faces. [See below]

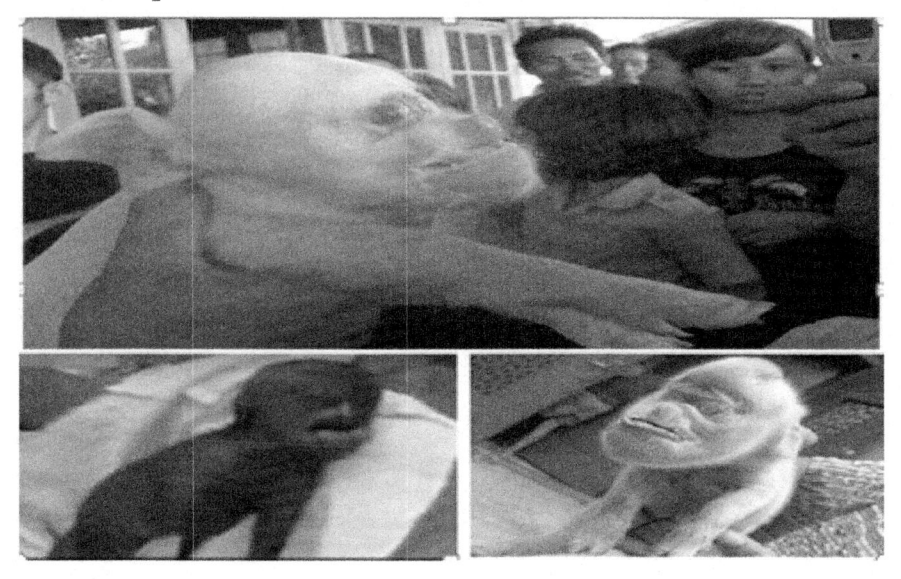

These are not made by inappropriate sexual conduct, but by something called Transhumanism. Possibly this transhumanism was what happened during the Bharata War. Too much experimenting and not enough control has started to become an epidemic. It was initiated for a somewhat noble idea that we could make human parts on animals and only kill animals to keep us alive longer. It wasn't started until 1926 when Russian scientists began inseminations of chimpanzees in Africa and in Russia. We are told the experiments were unsuccessful. Since then gene spicing has become a household word.

Genetic Manipulation

Today scientists are much more responsible in what they do about making new animals. Most of us have heard about the puppies, fish, cats, and mice built to glow in the dark [1 and 2 in collage]. Others of the more responsible experiments include the fruit-fly grown to have legs coming out where antenna were [3], featherless chickens [4], big eared pigs and those with human organs [5], a human ear growing out the back of a mouse [6], gigantic animals like the monster bull [7], the sheep born with a human head [8], the mouse implanted with "created" memories [9], the dog with a second dog torso "bonded" to it.[10].

I just saw in the news England has granted it's OK to modify human genes to make a better baby, and we now have made an animal that is about 40% human to allow retrieval of body parts. While all of this seems well regulated and scientific and all, just imagine where the Pleistocene scientists went with it as they even recreated entire Tyrannosaurus Rex, just like the Jurassic Park movies.

Both genetic and just plain weird manipulation of our bodies has occurred recently. From the current events, we can only imagine what freaks were made before the time of Adam. Greeks tell us of half human half-goat people and many others. Today we have made all types of wonderful monsters. You may remember seeing a fruit-fly that had a second pair of wings coming out where his eyes or the animal that eats oil in some class at college, but it has become so much worse. As an update to the animal that eats oil, it was never let free in the environment because everyone was afraid of what it might also do. Many "mistakes" were done that we don't know about, I'm sure. Images below left are the pictures of genetically altered puppies that glow in the dark and a mouse with an unusual ear growing out of his back, but we didn't stop there, because nakedness was on our minds.

Genetically Bred Nakedness

We are not talking about people here, but instead we get naked chickens. [See the last picture] These genetically engineered chickens grow faster in hot climates, contain less subcutaneous fat to hold the feathers, require less ventilation in the summer, and are cheaper to produce because they don't require plucking. [Oh yes did I mention they're ugly?]

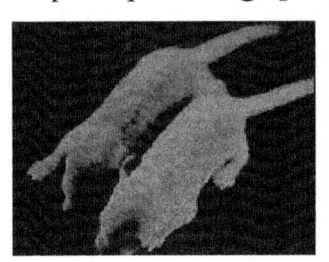

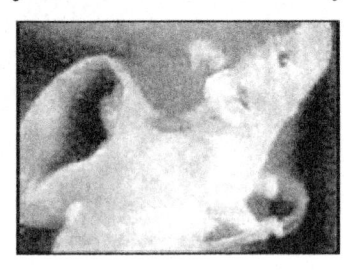

Pig Grows a Heart

Naked chickens are OK, but can we produce replacement organs? Today, Italian scientists have modified DNA to make a pig grow a human heart. Let's not get too worried, but remember, according to ancient texts around the world, God killed almost everyone during the heaven wars and again killed almost everyone before the worldwide flood. One of the main reasons during both instances was that <u>each group started making their own creations</u>. That is not to say that if we quit researching genetics that meteors won't hit us and wars won't happen, it only means that history repeats itself and the genetic breeding is a confirmation of the repeating.

Mouse Grows a Kidney

If pigs can do it, so can mice. The Israeli's copied the Italians and made a mouse grow a miniature human kidney by introducing stem cells. The kidney produced urine and the whole bit. It was just tiny. Researchers in the UK saw what the Israelis were doing and grabbed some rats to see what they could do. Now they have modified a rat to grow a larger brain. Anyone who has seen the Pinky and the Brain cartoons knows what will happen with these guys, but now it's not a cartoon.

Almost a Human

I read recently that these crazy scientists can now make an animal that is 15% human. They taut it as a great accomplishment, but I'm not too sure. There is no greater warning from ancient religious and historical texts than the warning against changing animals into other animals.

Glowing Rat Hair

In the United States, scientists said, "We can do something with those rats!" They mixed tropical fish and jellyfish DNA into mice DNA to make mice hair glow green, red, or blue.

That was pretty good, but one scientist said, "Let's turn them into robots."

Remote Control Rodents

As shown below, electrodes implanted into the brain and a remote control, force this rat to turn left, right, climb a tree, jump, and stop on command. Just think what the scientific community has in store for people.

Mechanical Brain Transplant

We don't have brain transplants YET, but in March 2003 prototypes of the world's first brain prosthesis; an artificial hippocampus, was revealed to the public. By using this electronic device, scientists believe that defects that come from stroke, epilepsy or Alzheimer's disease may be treatable. The device simply reads information the brain normally sends to the hippocampus and it then sends out signals similar to those generated in the hippocampus. It's sort of a drop in replacement. It will not only affect memory but also a person's mood, awareness and consciousness. It will make a "new person" and how much difference there will be is not known. The bioengineering cyberneticists hope it will be a better person and I do to. That hippocampus is a strange word isn't it? I'm glad God didn't make a mistake and put a hippopotamus in our brain. I also hope the geneticists don't make that mistake.

Modern Chimera-Genetics

Those are just a very few of the genetic manipulated events. Our modern genetic magic is truly amazing. Here are a few more of the thousands of genetic manipulated successes.

- *Manufactured tobacco that produces human blood components.*
- *Manufactured tooth decay bacteria that won't cause tooth decay*
- *Manufactured gene that eliminates muscular dystrophy in mice*
- *Created cardiomyopathic mice so they could try to cure this human only disease*
- *Manufactured skin that was transplanted onto 45% of a baby's bad skin.*
- *Manufactured worms that live 50% longer than others.*
- *Genetically altered blind dog that could see again*
- *Genetically altered sightless fish that now have eyes*
- *Produced bone from skin and gum tissue*
- *Genetically engineered ears on mice*
- *Developed an artificial drug that burns fat faster in mice*
- *Altered hair to make it glow different colors*
- *Genetically altered rabbit that glows under a black light.*
- *Genetically grown frog eyes and frog ears without a frog*
- *Genetically grown snake venom cells without a snake*
- *Produced a mouse with downs syndrome*
- *Altered a fish that grows faster, mates more often and his offspring that dies more quickly, showing that genetically manufactured animals could accidentally wipe out species.*

If that list is impressive, those are only a few of the things we know about. We can assume where there are a few successes, there are many mistakes. This list does show that cloned and manufactured animals and control of genetics are both becoming common place in something we call Trans-human Chimera.

Transhumanism

Transhumanism is modern genetic modification of humans. Since 2011 DARPA has provided millions of dollars in this type of bio-design to increase capabilities in soldiers. Add gorilla strength, cheetah speed etc. The one they are currently interested in is soldiers with genetic night vision like some of the deep sea animals. This goes way beyond what we imagined. We are used to genetically modified crops and drugs to cure cancer, but this is something else. In Britain, for instance, you can have a fetus developed to a specific sex, eye color and other capabilities. It's like getting a store bought baby. At one time this sort of thig must have gone too far. One report indicates Britain alone there were over 150 "fully developed" animal/human chimeras in 2012.

Let me show you some of the success that may be already done. Here is a cute bunny with human features. This Chimera was made in South America and filmed in 2011. Next to her is a frog-human chimera developed in 2010.

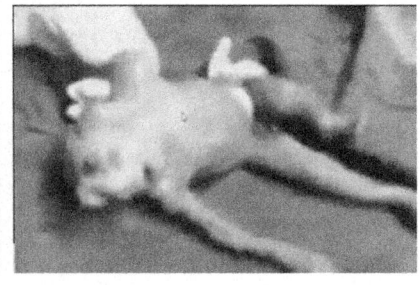

A German museum reportedly hatched a Gasosaurus theropod egg found in China that is supposedly still alive. [See next left]. In New Zealand they are attempting to clone a 100 year old Tasmanian Tiger fetus preserved in alcohol. [Next right]

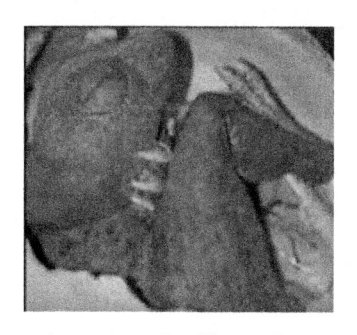

Don't even belive that some science experiment gone wrong did not make a huge population of Ape-like humans and the Chimpanzee. As described in numerous places as chimpanzees are the closest DNA match, so even a slight nuclear mutation could have set the events off even without scinetists. Please do not disregard this information. I think this imformation is not being disemenated well in our classrooms and with that, let's recap and make some determinations.

Conclusions

Hopefully you at least learned a few things or are mad enough to go investigate the suppositions established in this book. Some of the more important elements are listed below.

- Apes did not simply form from an amoeba sitting on a stone that was hit by lightning in fact; lightning did not put sugars together in any form that would resemble DNA that could eventually establish life. No animal was. There is something unknown about the establishment of life that goes beyond complex sugars associated with DNA. Animals had a creator that initiated everything. That does not mean that the creator created all animals. He did not. For that we go to the ancient humans
- Humans walked with dinosaurs and instigated a massive assault on a place called Heaven by the end of the Cretaceous Period. They had created the dinosaurs, but lost the war. After the war, things were hard and the ancient human survivors began searching for ways to make their life easier. The best way was to have other people to do the work so they created some by combining DNA of already created animals with different genes or even by combinant structures embedding their own DNA.
- We can imagine the first modified mammals were little better than the rats, but soon they began to look more and more like the apes of today and even people.
- While these scientists were good at changing positions of amino acids in chromosomal chains, they were not creators in the strictest sense so there were limitations to

what they could do. God helped them from time to time by creating new forms of human. One on what the Bible terms as the 6th period human was, most likely the Homo Erectus. This was during the Tertiary Period of the Earth.
- Wow! What a difference. This guy spoke, ran, make weapons, and pretty much was like we are today, but there were limitations as far as the ancient humans thought so they set about changing the new human. We can believe some of the modifications were the beginnings of Gorillas, Orangutans, etc.
- When that was not as successful as they would like, God stepped in again and made the new human we call Cro Magnon, 40 thousand years ago.
- Some massive mutations occurred 10 to 12 thousand years ago and the record is locked in our DNA. Possibly chimpanzees were designed or mutated at this time, but we looked at a different possibility.
- After the Pleistocene Extinction, civilization, bioengineering, and war were reestablished.
- Another massive war resulted in another huge increase in mutation in humans. This time there was a substantial reduction in capability and evolution. In fact, somehow, DNA was disrupted so much that a large group became Ape-like.
- For as long as 25 hundred years this misshapen group of ape-like people were accepted into society, but the DNA was somewhat unstable.
- Chimpanzees may have been one of the unfortunate offshoots from the human mutations of this time. We know that chimpanzee mutations are substantially more often that human mutation showing the instability of their DNA

God did not make the ape!

About The Author

Steve Preston is a long lime author of scientific, esoteric facts. The books focus on the painful truths rather than whitewashed details that make us comfortable. If you are interested in the truth instead of comfort, please continue to read and, while you are at it, review other works by Mr. Preston as shown below.

Kingdoms Before the Flood	*Races of Men*
Scythians Conquered Ireland	*The Second Creation of Man*
Behind the Tower of Babel	*A Closer Look at Ancient History*
Ancient History of Flying	*Man After The Flood*
When Giants Ruled the Earth	*The Antediluvian War Years*
Lizard People	*Driven Underground*
Who Really Discovered the Americas?	*The Creation of Adam and Eve*
Disgusting Display	*Mysterious Pyramids*
The First Creation of Man	*World War Zero*
America's Civil War Lie	*A New View of Modern History*
Allah' God of the Moon	*Anthropic Reality*
Living On Mars, Venus, and the Moon	*Our 10-Dimensional Universe*
Vibrational Matter	*Victory of the Earth*
Walk Through Time or a Wall	*Not from Space*
Mystery of Photons and Light	*DNA of Our Ancestors*
Anakim Gods	*20th Century To The End Of Time*
Adam's First Wife	*Creation and Death of Dinosaurs*
Biophotonics and Healing	*Four Armageddons*
Closer Look At Genesis	*World War Before*
Moses Saved Egypt	*The Antichrist*

Self, Soul, Spirit   *Errors in Understanding*
Mysteries of the Exodus   *Retiming the Earth*
God Didn't Make The Ape   *Six Deaths of Man*
Meaning of Life and Light   *Why Rome Fought the Berserkers*
Releasing Your Consciousness   *Awaken the Departed*
History Confirmed By The Bible   *The Bad Side of Lincoln*
Sex Crazed Angels   *Life Resonance*
Terror of Global Warming   *Vampires among Us*
Great American Quiz   *American School Disaster*
World War with Heaven   *Promote the General Welfare*

Printed in Great Britain
by Amazon